STEP

—

PURSUING YOUR DREAMS IN THE MIDST OF EVERYDAY LIFE

—

CHRIS CAPEHART

ISBN: 978-0-9970298-0-2 (soft cover)

ISBN: 978-0-9970298-1-9 (epub)

Library of Congress Control Number: 2015919608

First edition: December 2015

Published in the United States of America

1 2 3 4 5 6 7 8 9 10

WELCOME TO YOUR FIRST STEP

This is more than just a regular book that you buy and put on the shelf to collect dust. It was born to travel. If you are the first person to receive this book please register it by filling in the form on the next page. Then, go to ChrisCapehart.co and register it. When you're done take a step and pass it along to someone who needs it. If you are the recipient of this book being passed along please fill in the section that applies to you so we can see where the book goes and how it's affecting lives around the world. You can also go to ChrisCapehart.co and let us know that the book has been passed to you. This way there will always be a log of where every book is and has gone. You'll be able to see how your step has traveled around the world and is affecting the lives of many!

NAME YOUR BOOK

(Naming this book will help you keep track of it as it takes steps along its journey. Have fun and be creative. ex: My Path to Awesome)

First Reader

Name ——————————————————————

Date ——————————————————————

Location ——————————————————————

A Step I've Taken ——————————————————————

Second Reader

Name ——————————————————————

Date ——————————————————————

Location ——————————————————————

A Step I've Taken ——————————————————————

Third Reader

Name ——————————————————————

Date ——————————————————————

Location ——————————————————————

A Step I've Taken ——————————————————————

Fourth Reader

Name _____

Date _____

Location _____

A Step I've Taken _____

Fifth Reader

Name _____

Date _____

Location _____

A Step I've Taken _____

Sixth Reader

Name _____

Date _____

Location _____

A Step I've Taken _____

Seventh Reader

Name _____

Date _____

Location _____

A Step I've Taken _____

To my grandfather. His example started all of this in me.

To my beautiful wife, Amy, who supports and encourages me to pursue my dreams with complete confidence. My partner in life who I could never imagine being without.

To my daughter, Avery, who brings a smile and purpose to everything I do.

To God, who will take this wherever it may go.

CONTENTS

1
ONE ROW AT A TIME

We don't know each other, but I'll dare to guess we have at least one thing in common: Who we are today is not who we want to be tomorrow.

You wouldn't have picked up this book if it weren't true. There is still so much I want to achieve in this life. I want to be a better person. I want to leave a bigger legacy. I want to build something great. I want my life to have impact beyond what it would if today were my last day.

As big as my dreams may be, my doubts are often bigger. Does my past define my future? Am I too old? Am I too young? Do I really have what it takes?

My hunch is you've probably been plagued by questions like these. Questions are good, but sometimes we don't even bother to ask them—we jump straight to telling ourselves: I'm too old, I'm too young, I'm not smart enough. I could never do that.

If we do this long enough, we lose all hope to dream. We don't dare to reach for something bigger for fear that we'll just be disappointed. The moment a hopeful thought seeps up, we slam it back down like a game of whack-a-mole. We may even pat ourselves on the back for not allowing that annoying little dream to ruin our day. *Take that, nagging feeling! I'll teach you not to interrupt my comfortable life.* The worst part is, we usually don't even realize we're doing this. The big dreams just seem so big that we don't know what else to do.

It's time to change the way we look at accomplishing our dreams.

My grandfather Stan did just that. He changed the course of his life, and his family's, for generations to come. He wasn't famous. He didn't hold some magical ability. He didn't come from a well-to-do family. Honestly, he didn't have anything special going for him.

Stan Goss was the son of an Arkansas sharecropper, born in a small rural town just before the Great Depression. The Goss family worked tirelessly, but they still barely got by. Growing up surrounded by such extreme poverty motivated Stan to escape

"

It's time to change the way we look at accomplishing our dreams.

CHRISCAPEHART.CO

Snap it, remember it, share it.

#STEPBOOK

What does this statement mean to you?
Write it down.

_____

_____

_____

_____

CHRISCAPEHART.CO

Think about it, wrestle with it, do it.
#STEPBOOK

and create a better life.

Stan found his opportunity in the U.S. Army. Enlisting provided Stan with a way to see the world while also paying the bills. It was a chance at a new life.

Stan signed up when he was 22 and immediately received his orders to Hawaii, but before he was deployed, he tied the knot with his sweetheart, Shirley. If you ever meet Shirley, she'll tell you he was head over heels from the moment he saw her. She is quite the character; just a few minutes with her and you'll have a story to tell. Stan, on the other hand, is a bit more reserved.

One evening, Stan and Shirley heard a knock at the door. It was a salesman offering a beautiful set of stainless-steel cookware. Turns out, he was in luck, because Shirley loved to cook. The salesman did a good job convincing Shirley that *this* was the set she needed to buy. Unfortunately, although the Army provided a steady paycheck, it wasn't substantial— around $200 a month, which was barely enough to get by. The set cost around $210, and they had the option to pay for it in installments of $12 a month. But they couldn't possibly afford to buy this luxury . . . even on a payment plan.

The salesman was dead-set on persuading Stan and Shirley to purchase the cookware. "It's only $12 a month!" he kept saying.

Finally, in a fit of frustration, Shirley placed all of their paystubs and bills on the table and said, "If you can find the extra money, we'll buy it!

The numbers just didn't work.

"OK," he said, "you don't have the money."

"That's what I've been trying to tell you." Shirley shot him a look of triumph.

But the salesman wasn't ready to give up.

"Shirley, if you can get five people to buy a set, yours is free. You just have to buy the $10 sales kit to get started."

Stan, who hadn't said a word this whole time, suddenly piped up: "I can do that."

"That would be the biggest waste of $10 ever!" Shirley laughed with a hoot. She wasn't convinced her knight in shining armour had the skills to pull it off. After all, he wasn't very conversational.

But Stan had already made up his mind and bought the sales kit right there. He wanted Shirley to have the cookware because he knew all too well that "a happy wife equals a happy life."

Even more so, he was confident he could earn a free set because of some principles he had learned from his years growing up on a farm.

Within a few short weeks, Stan found five other couples to purchase the cookware and then proudly presented a set to Shirley for their own home. But he didn't stop there.

Stan continued telling people about the cookware and became one of the top salesmen for that company. He started making $1,000 a month on top of his $200 Army salary. And he did it all after he got off work at 5:00 p.m. each day! With one decision, Stan turned the tide for his entire family.

After his service with the Army, Stan went on to be pretty successful with several other companies before starting two multimillion-dollar businesses of his own. Shirley happily admits that she has been eating her words for more than 50 years now!

A lady once asked Stan what he did to become successful. He responded with a question: "Have you ever planted a garden?"

"Yes," she said.

"Did you plant a row of corn in that garden?"

Again, she answered, "Yes."

"Was it a good row of corn?"

Chuckling a bit, she said that yes, it was a good row of corn. Stan told her: "Then you already know everything I know about becoming successful. You do it one row at a time."

"One row at a time." This phrase has been ringing in my head since the first time I heard it. I was a child at the time, but the story behind that statement made me believe I could do *anything*.

In fact, I'm sure you've probably heard several variations of this advice before:

How do you eat an elephant? One bite at a time.

Slow and steady wins the race.

Don't bite off more than you can chew.

Rome wasn't built in a day.

At their core, these popular adages remind us that tackling a big endeavor requires time, patience and, most importantly, *consistent incremental progress.*

If Sir Edmund Hillary and Tenzing Norgay had never placed one foot in front of the other and actually taken that first step up Mount Everest, they wouldn't have been the first people to reach its summit.

If Rosa Parks hadn't refused to move from her seat on a bus, equal rights may not be a reality in the United States today.

If Walt Disney hadn't asked that first bank for a loan and then kept trying again and again, he would have never found the 300th bank that ultimately funded his dream of a magical park, which has now become Disney World.

If Dorothy hadn't slipped on those ruby slippers and taken that first step onto the yellow brick road, she would have never reached the Emerald City or defeated the Wicked Witch of the West.

If I hadn't powered up my laptop, opened up a document, and started typing that first sentence, you wouldn't be reading this book right now.

No matter what your dream, your task, or your goal, just about *anything* can be accomplished . . . if you take it one step (or row) at a time.

Now, if you're anything like me, you've probably set a goal at some point in your life, and despite your best intentions, failed miserably at achieving it.

NO MATTER WHAT YOUR DREAM, YOUR TASK, OR YOUR GOAL, JUST ABOUT ANYTHING CAN BE ACCOMPLISHED . . . IF YOU TAKE IT ONE STEP (OR ROW) AT A TIME.

Because of your past failure, maybe you feel embarrassed about trying again. Or maybe you've never even tried giving your dreams a shot because you're afraid you'll never reach them no matter how long you try.

Maybe you feel this way because of something someone has said to you . . . or even worse, because of what you've told yourself. Over time, all those voices in your head have subtly influenced what you do and ultimately shaped who you've become.

Whether we like to admit it or not, it's hard to silence those voices and believe we have what it takes to achieve our dreams. So here's what I want you to walk away from this book knowing above all else: You can change your life one step at a time. Your past does not define who you can become. Whether young, old, or in between, your age doesn't have to limit your opportunity. Your level of education or amount of life experience is not a ceiling that blocks you from rising to a new level of success. You can choose to believe a lie or you can choose to create your own story starting now.

I know a step can seem pretty insignificant, and it's true— one step by itself won't get you very far at all. *However*, when you follow that one step with another step, and then another, and then another . . . suddenly, you look back and realize that what you once thought was impossible is now within your grasp.

I think a quote often attributed to Saint Francis of Assisi sums it up well: "Start by doing what's necessary, then do what's possible, and suddenly you are doing the impossible."

Still . . . Almost sounds *too* simple, doesn't it? Of course it does. But see what happens if you try it. You just might change your life.

"START BY DOING WHAT'S NECESSARY, THEN DO WHAT'S POSSIBLE, AND SUDDENLY YOU ARE DOING THE IMPOSSIBLE."

SAINT FRANCIS OF ASSISI

This book has altered my life in many ways. Writing it was a journey of using the principles inside. This book is a product of the Step process. I take each principle and show how what you're reading was made possible by the very thing that you're reading. The proof really is in the pudding.

We'll also follow my grandfather Stan's journey throughout these pages and see how he leveraged the Step principles in every one of his endeavors. We'll meet others, too, like Chase and Cambryn Willsey, whose story of paying off debt is truly inspirational, and Jon and Trina Mitchell, who teamed up with fellow entrepreneurs in a surprising way to make their dream come true.

As we follow these journeys, my hope is that you can see yourself in these stories and see how you can apply these principles to your own life. And don't worry—I won't leave you hanging with stories alone. You'll walk away from each chapter with concrete ideas for implementing the Step principles into your life, no matter where you find yourself on your journey.

2
STEP: THE MINDSET

As a man thinketh, so is he.

If you can dream it, you can achieve it.

I think I can, I think I can, I think I can.

Most people have heard one if not all of these sayings at some point in their life. No matter how it's said, the message is the same: If you believe in yourself, you can accomplish anything. There have been countless studies and books written on this subject. The idea is littered throughout history and religion. It is one of the most timeless principles, and for good reason. Belief is as essential to achieving your goals as your heart is essential to proper blood flow throughout your body.

Finding belief when you don't have it can be a bit difficult. When you believe in yourself you can accomplish anything, but what happens when you don't believe? Is it possible to change your mind? Hold on to that question for just a second.

We all come from different backgrounds and different perspectives that have helped shape our belief in ourselves. It would take an entire book—or more—to explore how our beliefs are formed, but the fact is, it doesn't matter. We can't change where we've come from, but we can change where we're going.

So the answer to the question above is a resounding "Yes!" You can change what you believe you are capable of achieving and that's where we start.

WE CAN'T CHANGE WHERE WE'VE COME FROM, BUT WE CAN CHANGE WHERE WE'RE GOING.

What You Say Matters More Than You May Think

What you believe is reflected in what you say and your words can help shape your thinking. This is not a mythic concept and I'm not suggesting that you wake every morning, walk outside, and tell the world you are [fill in the blank].

Just for fun I'm going to fill in the blank . . .

. . . The sexiest person alive . . . Stronger than the Hulk . . . Smarter than your boss . . . Richer than Bill Gates.

I am, however, suggesting that you consider the power of positive thinking and speaking. I've heard countless stories about adults who believe they will never amount to anything because of something a parent, teacher, or bully said to them when they were children. If anyone doubts whether words influence belief, just think about how many of us allow them to set our limits.

If some—let me just call it how it is—stupid people can shape what we believe about ourselves with meaningless words that they never gave another thought to, why can't we shape our lives with an even stronger force?

I would like to take a second to talk about the amazing miracle that is you. You are unique and were created with a special sequence of this stuff called DNA. There is no one in the entire world that has or will ever have the same DNA as you. Have you ever thought about that? Have you ever taken the time to consider that you are special and that there may be something bigger at work than chance? Is it possible that your creation was planned by something or someone bigger?

You are special. You are unique. You can accomplish your dreams. You can create a better life for your family. You can lose that weight. You can start that business. You are a success.

There are people who are proud of you. There is a community of people who have overcome the destructive words and beliefs spoken to them. You have what it takes to change your life and you will change the world one step at a time.

You can change what you believe about yourself. You just have to do it in steps. I encourage you to find the counterstatement to every belief that has held you back. Anytime your mind starts to dwell on that false belief, say out loud the counter.

This is the first step to changing what you believe.

Let me give you a few examples:

If your thought is: I can't do _____

Say: I can do _____

If your thought is: I don't have what it takes to do _____

Say: I have what it takes to do _____

If you come from a broken home like I did, you may have a strong desire to create a different future for your family, but deep down you may not believe you are capable of being the husband, wife, dad, or mom that you wish you had growing up.

My dad was a pastor. He cheated on my mom and was publicly confronted in front of the entire church. Unfortunately, this wasn't his first mistake and it wouldn't be his last. When my dad's short life came to an end at the age of 58, he had been married four times. None of these marriages were successful, and there's a good chance that even if the cancer hadn't taken his life, he would have continued to struggle in this area.

My dad may not have been the picture of perfection as a husband, but he did love me very much and for that I'm eternally grateful. There are a good many things I learned from my dad that have shaped the man I am today. I will share those in the following pages of this book.

I want to be faithful to my wife forever, but there is a force that tries to tell me I will be just like my dad when it comes to fidelity. But I have the choice to believe something different. I can change what I allow myself to believe, and it starts by simply telling myself, "I will be faithful." I can confront any thought or situation that challenges my goal by speaking my belief and taking the actions that align with it. It's all about getting into the right mindset.

Find the Opportunity in Every Failure

Past experience is a major factor that shapes belief. It's been said that experience is the greatest teacher. If this is true, but our experience has been failure, wouldn't it stand to reason that if we try again we will most likely fail? Yes, but only if you focus on the failure instead of on the lessons you could have learned.

The feeling of failure is so painful that we often steer clear of a second try, or maybe it's a third or a fourth. It kills our belief. Facing failure is never an easy task, but it's one worth pursuing. The challenge is to put yourself in the right mindset so you can tackle the obstacle in a new way. My grandfather was selling cookware door to door in Hawaii. Many of the doors he knocked on didn't open, but he needed to connect with the people in those homes. How could he turn every unanswered door into an opportunity to provide for his family?

Instead of counting each unanswered door as a failure, he looked for a different way to approach the situation. He recorded his sales pitch about the cookware on a vinyl record. Then, he placed it in a bright red bag and hung it on the doors that didn't open. He left a note saying he would return the next day to pick it up. Records weren't cheap to produce so he had a real reason to come back.

He would come back to the house when he stated, knock on the door and politely ask to retrieve his vinyl record. It worked. Those closed doors turned into new connections, and in many cases, new customers. In fact, it worked so well that his company asked him to teach other salesmen what he was doing.

I don't know how many doors my grandfather knocked on that never opened, but he never let failure (or the appearance of it) stop him from believing in himself.

Experience with failure can help you win the next time around. If you have been letting a bad experience stop you from moving forward take a few minutes and ask yourself:

What can I learn from my past experience attempting _____?

Based on what I've learned, what three things would I do differently next time?

Just a year out of college, two of my best friends and I started the biggest venture of our lives to date. The name was ROOV.com. We were trying to create a place for people of faith to connect with like-minded individuals as they pursued their goals and dreams. At the time we were attending a church with almost 20,000 members. We were young entrepreneurs and had a difficult time finding other people like ourselves. We thought technology could help.

We were able to raise a little over $600,000 to go after our big goal. We hired a team, worked to be as lean as possible, and ultimately launched what we believed was an amazing tool. We had some success too, thousands of people joined and we landed partnerships with major organizations.

We had leveraged everything to make this dream a reality and on the outside it looked pretty successful, but . . .

We weren't growing our user base fast enough. And although we had repeat visitors, we didn't have enough. We'd spent the bulk of our resources building the online platform from scratch, but when it came to the end of our funding, we weren't able to raise the additional capital needed to keep the business going. The story ends with us having to shut the company down and lay off our entire team.

For quite a while after this experience I was scared to take another big risk. I was having a hard time believing that I had what it took to build a great company. I was focusing on the failure instead of on the lessons. I honestly thought I'd done everything possible to save ROOV.com and there was no way I could be successful in the future because I couldn't have done anything differently.

I should have been asking myself what I could learn from that experience that would help me the next time I wanted to start something. When I finally did, here is what I learned:

Listen to my advisors. Our board had always advised us to charge organizations for our service and give each group a branded version. We fought this advice tooth and nail. At the time I held the strong belief that we should offer our service for free and make money through advertising. I didn't want each organization to have an individual, closed-off environment. I thought everything should be open and I could not see how we could accomplish our vision if it wasn't that way. Neither view was necessarily wrong, but looking back I believe that the model we chose was part of the reason we weren't successful. I should have been willing to shift my vision when it became clear that our setup wasn't working. Several competitors in the space have popped up over the years and have been profitable following the very model that our board wanted us to use. With regard to accomplishing our vision, we could have started with closed environments that one day would have been opened up. I had a hard time seeing how a slight shift in perspective may have been the critical component to accomplishing the vision at all.

Next time I should place more value on my advisors' opinions and trust their guidance. If I can't do that, then I probably shouldn't have them as advisors.

Build small (or lean) and test constantly. This is a common practice in today's software world, but it wasn't at the time. We believed we needed to build every feature to accomplish our one goal of connecting people online to get them offline. We spent around 75% of our money building supporting features and about 25% building the actual things we wanted to achieve. And we barely tested. We tested when we launched and by that time we had spent so much of our money that we couldn't properly iterate. I guess we thought we knew it all.

Never stop raising. We learned the hard way that a start-up should never stop raising money. We thought we had raised more than enough to get the traction we would need for a second round of funding. We hadn't and so we didn't.

We learned much more, but the point is that after discovering these three lessons, my fear of starting a new business wasn't quite so bad. I had a concrete understanding of why our business had failed and I could change my approach going forward.

My belief in myself started to be restored. Let experience teach you, not stop you, from pursuing your dreams. Don't let your failure dictate your belief; let it guide all your future attempts.

Find Your First Step

We can spend a lot of time giving ourselves pep talks, or pulling lessons out of past failures, but nothing is more effective in building our belief in ourselves than *doing*. What can you do today that would fly in the face of any negative words spoken, past experience, or limitation you're imposing on yourself?

There are likely some powerful forces shaping your beliefs. Maybe someone in your family told you you're just like your dad or your mom. Even though they may have been referring to your appearance, or a great talent you inherited, that statement might limit your beliefs about who you can be. Most of us harbor these kinds of negative, long-held beliefs, and they're nothing to be ashamed of. Your challenge is to just find the first step that will move you in a new direction.

We can't change years of thinking and believing overnight, but we can start with a small step toward changing what we believe by changing what we say about ourselves.

Remember, this is a step. One step leads to another and to another until we look back and see the mile we have run.

You can't afford to let negative thoughts linger in your mind. You may not believe what you're saying at first, but here is a trick to help: Break it down into steps. We will talk at length about how to do this in the next chapter, but let me whet your appetite.

REMEMBER, THIS IS A STEP. ONE STEP LEADS TO ANOTHER AND TO ANOTHER UNTIL WE LOOK BACK AND SEE THE MILE WE HAVE RUN.

If you have a hard time believing you can lose 100 pounds, give yourself something you *can* believe. That will be your first step. For instance: I can eat one healthy meal today. That is believable, and if you can eat one healthy meal today, you can eat one tomorrow and the next day. Once you start to give yourself something you can believe in, you will find that believing you can lose 100 pounds won't be as hard because you've already proven your ability with your first step. Whenever the negative thoughts start to creep in, you'll have something new to motivate you: your steps—those you've taken, and those you're about to take.

It's critical for you to believe in what you're doing. It's too easy to give up when things get tough if you don't truly believe that your goal is important. But there's a difference between *believing in the goal* and *believing that you can do it*. If you can't quite believe you can achieve the thing you desire, find the thing you do believe you can do and start there.

I had a hard time believing I could find time to write a book, but I could believe I could write for two hours a week. After convincing myself that I could write a little bit every week I was on my way. Several weeks in, I realized I can do this! I started with what I could believe and that led me to a new level of belief in my own abilities.

IF YOU CAN'T QUITE BELIEVE YOU CAN ACHIEVE THE THING YOU DESIRE, FIND THE THING YOU DO BELIEVE YOU CAN DO AND START THERE.

Is it really possible to accomplish anything as long as you believe? I'm not going to attempt to answer that question right now, but I can say that without belief, there is almost a 100% chance that your dream isn't possible.

Find the step within your goal that you do believe you can accomplish and start there. You can change the way you view yourself. This is the start to changing your life.

3
THE PROVERBIAL MILE: WHAT STOPS US FROM STEPPING

We're often distracted by the "proverbial mile" that stands between us and our goal. It's sometimes our biggest opponent because the enormity of the work needed to achieve our dream is crippling. When we focus on the mile, we lose sight of the step. When we lose sight of the step, we don't move. And when we don't move, our dreams, our desires, and potentially our destiny go unfulfilled.

I've found myself stuck by the proverbial mile several times while writing this book. I'm not surprised—we're just more accustomed to looking at the mile than at the step in front of us. It's a natural part of what we do. In fact, we have to look at the mile. It's typically the first thing we do when trying to size up our ability to achieve a goal. If we never looked at the mile, we would never know what it takes to get where we want to go. The problem is not in looking at the mile, but getting stuck focusing on the mile. Our brains are constantly trying to evaluate where we are in relation to the mile and what's still left to accomplish our goals. Too often the mile can feel overwhelming, and that's why we have to train ourselves to think and act differently, focusing on one step at a time.

The mile (aka our ferocious enemy) is not as big and bad as he may seem. But don't take him for granted. He'll jump up and have you stuck before you realize what's happening. In fact, his job is to trick us into believing we can't accomplish the thing we desire therefore rendering us stagnant. He's a liar.

My wife and I were recently watching one of our favorite shows, *NCIS*, and one of the main characters, Ducky, made this statement: "When you are overwhelmed, do something you know you can accomplish and suddenly you won't be quite so overwhelmed."

I love this statement. It sums up a lot of what I'm talking about in this chapter and in this book. It's a powerful principle yet so simple to understand. Typically, in those moments of being paralyzed by the overwhelming number of tasks we believe it will take to accomplish our goals, we simply can't move or can't decide how to move.

"WHEN YOU ARE OVERWHELMED, DO SOMETHING YOU KNOW YOU CAN ACCOMPLISH AND SUDDENLY YOU WON'T BE QUITE SO OVERWHELMED."

DUCKY, *NCIS*

We can't move because we're looking at the wrong thing. *We're looking at everything we need to accomplish instead of looking at the one thing we can accomplish.*

The mile got the best of me while I was writing this book. These few paragraphs I'm writing now are actually a part of my second draft. I blazed through the first six months taking step after step until I hit a sticking point. I'll share more about this sticking point in a later chapter.

Though I had a complete draft of the book after those six months, one small setback refocused my brain on the mile instead of the step. I hate to admit it, but I've spent the last few months being a bit overwhelmed by how to move the book forward. Just the other night I sat in my office for an hour and didn't do anything. I couldn't figure out what to do next.

I'm teaching this concept and even I struggle with it! I can get overwhelmed even after I've made a ton of progress. The great news is that the biggest setbacks can be overcome by shifting your focus back to the smallest step.

This kind of refocusing is not a one-time occurrence. The mile will tempt you again and again, and that's OK. When you're overwhelmed, stop and think about one small thing you *can* do now. Then make that your only goal. Look at it in the way that most of us look at buying a house or a car. Though the large item's sticker price is far out of reach, we tend to focus on the monthly payment. That's how you should tackle your mile. You know it's there, you understand it, and you figure out the monthly payment you can manage so you can start chipping away.

WE'RE LOOKING AT EVERYTHING WE NEED TO ACCOMPLISH INSTEAD OF LOOKING AT THE ONE THING WE CAN ACCOMPLISH.

When I was younger I was very athletic. I played basketball, ran track, and watched what I ate. Even after college I kept a pretty steady regimen. Then I married my beautiful wife and started trading some of my gym time for hanging out on the couch with her. While that's a noble thing, unfortunately, my nobility packed on another 15 pounds. It shocked me a bit when I woke up one morning, looked in the mirror, and realized I wasn't so slim!

I quickly kicked in gear and started getting up early and working out hard. I was young and it wasn't too long until I was back in shape. Fast-forward a few years to my wife's pregnancy. I tried so hard to eat well, but it didn't last. I needed to be sympathetic to my wife and help her eat all of that junk food our baby needed to grow. Needless to say, I gained some extra weight.

My baby girl is a year old now and I still have that extra weight. I had spent the last year and a half not eating right or working out, because "I just don't have the time, and it's too big of a commitment." I kept telling myself I didn't want to start working out unless I could do it right.

I figured if I worked out hard and ate a bit better, I could lose the extra pounds in three months. But then I kept trying to psyche myself up for three months of sacrifice, and it just wasn't happening. While reflecting on my impending challenge, I stayed on the couch eating pizza. I figured I'd better get as much rest and food for now as I could, because "when" (read: "if") I commit, it was going to be *tough!* I kept telling myself: "Only three months of sacrifice, *then* I can maintain." Even though I hadn't maintained the last two times I did this, I was sure this time would be different. Why I thought so, I don't know. Perhaps I was out to prove Einstein's definition of insanity: doing the same thing over and over and expecting different results.

Three months of sacrifice was my focus (my proverbial mile), when I should have been thinking about 10 minutes a day (my step). Ten minutes doesn't sound that bad, but it doesn't sound that impactful either. Let me challenge your thinking when it comes to small steps.

Ten minutes a day will give you 10 times the results of zero minutes. Compound that 10 *times* over 30 days and you are 10 to the 30th power closer to your goal. That sounds pretty incredible when you think about it. We just took the proverbial mile and broke it into one small step that has significantly more impact than it seems at face value. It definitely has more impact than doing nothing. And nothing is what most people will do.

Don't do nothing! Nothing breeds nothing! Only do nothing if you want nothing!

I'm currently back on my daily regimen. I work out 15 minutes a day. Interestingly enough, the more consistent I am with 15 minutes the more I want to do a few more minutes. This is the principle of momentum that we will discuss in Chapter 6.

. . . And what about eating right? I'll be honest, the idea of eating salad, chia seeds, and vegetables for every meal is my big hurdle. It's more like two proverbial miles! I've done it, though. One time I willed myself to eat almost perfectly healthy for two months. I went cold turkey one day and changed my entire diet. I lost weight, felt great, but about as quickly as I started,

I stopped, and a few months later I gained the weight back.

I'm once again faced with the challenge of overhauling the way I eat. However, every time I'm about to start there is a trip to Cracker Barrel or In-N-Out Burger and I realize that I'm not so committed to this lifestyle of sacrifice. Just like with working out, I need a step and for me it's pretty simple. One good meal a day is where I start. It's not quite so intimidating. Some might substitute a water for a Coke, or fruit for chips. We just have to break our miles into steps. Steps are achievable and repeatable. The more steps we take the closer we get to living the life we want.

When I was young, I heard personal development expert Bob Proctor say you have to break your goals down to the ridiculous. For instance, to go a mile you have to travel 1,760 yards, or 5,280 feet (that's about 5,280 steps). We can even go further: A mile has 63,360 inches and you have to travel every one of those inches if you want to reach a mile. I sure like the idea of inches over miles.

I've mentioned writing a book, working out, and eating right, but this principle applies in almost every situation. Just think about my grandfather Stan Goss and his simple principle for success in sales. He focused on the one thing he knew he could do: talk to people. He knew if he did that enough times he would find himself earning the success he desired.

This notion also applies at multiple points in your journey. Every day, you have to choose to take the step with the mile staring you in the face. Each of us will struggle with different parts of the journey. For example, I'm good at starting while others may be better at finishing. I tend to get distracted by the mile farther down the journey while you may be distracted more at the beginning of yours.

No matter where you struggle with the mile, the principle remains the same. Get your eye on the step. Take the step even when it seems futile. Remember, *taking a step toward your goal is infinitely more powerful than not taking a step at all.*

We each have an incredible ability to accomplish our dreams. My goal is to get you to believe the same thing. If you can believe you can move an inch, I can take you a mile.

Throughout this book, I will help you map out your steps and regularly check whether you're on the right path. That second part is critical because Step is not about blind action, but purposeful and consistent action in the right direction.

What big challenge has been holding you back from moving forward in your work, marriage, dreams, or in any area of your life? What step can you take today to get closer to where you want to be tomorrow? Quit pondering the journey to the top of the mountain and just get to base camp!

Breaking Down the Proverbial Mile

That big challenge that's been holding you back? Let's break it down. Let's look at the impossible and figure out what's possible right now.

But before we start breaking down the proverbial mile, I want to be clear on what this exercise is—and what it isn't. It's not a way of cataloging every single step necessary for a complex project. You can't take something as intricate as, say, starting a business and capture every moving detail in a single line of steps. But you *can* look at something huge and distill it down to the first set of steps you need to get started. Remember: The goal is *consistent incremental progress*. That's it. Just focus on the immediate road in front of you for now.

As you progress, you can use this principle any time you're stuck. Something like starting a business will have several proverbial miles lurking within it, some more complicated than others. Just break them down so you can keep going.

The inverse is true for simpler goals, like eating healthy or exercising. You can break the whole mile into one linear set of steps—or even just one step on repeat. Write every day. Eat one healthy meal a day. Work out for 15 minutes each day. Simple or complex, you still need to break the thing down. This part is fun because you can use a formula to figure out your steps.

> "

Step is not about blind action, but purposeful and consistent action in the right direction.

CHRISCAPEHART.CO

Snap it, remember it, share it.

#STEPBOOK

What does this statement mean to you?
Write it down.

_____

_____

_____

_____

CHRISCAPEHART.CO

Think about it, wrestle with it, do it.
#STEPBOOK

Yes, you can actually plug that scary, overwhelming thing into a formula that will spit out the answers for you. My favorite formula for this exercise comes from the computer science world and uses one of the most common logic expressions: the *if–then* statement.

Don't worry if you're not computer savvy. This will be painless. In fact, you might understand programming better than you thought possible.

Here's how it works:

If _____ [insert condition] . . .

Then _____ [insert command]

Here's an example:

If [I want to own a house] . . .

Then [I need to buy a house]

Pretty basic, right? It's logical and that's why they call it a logic or logical expression. Let's take this same example and expand it.

If [I want to own a house] . . .

Then [I need to buy a house]

If [I need to buy a house] . . .

Then [I need to save money for a down payment]

If [I need to save money for a down payment] . . .

Then [I need to lower my monthly expenses]

If [I need to find ways to lower my monthly expenses] . . .

Then [I need to eat out less]

or

Then [I need to be more efficient with my electricity consumption]

or

Then [I need to consider renting my current place on Airbnb]

Most of us have probably gone through this thought process without being so deliberate. In fact, we do it every day. We are constantly assessing what's needed to accomplish the task in front of us, then doing those things. It's called being logical. However, getting a better understanding of how you can jump-start the logical side of your brain when you're having a hard time is a nice tool.

In the example above, we found three very attainable steps to take toward saving money for buying a house. You might be thinking this is all pretty obvious, and it is. The trick is to apply this logic to the goals we've had a hard time breaking down.

When my wife and I were first married, we were barely earning enough to cover our monthly expenses. However, we had five financial goals that we were committed to and we wanted to continue working toward them even though our situation wasn't the greatest. Our five goals were:

1. Paying off debt

2. Future kid account: saving a $10,000 safety net for when we had our first child

3. Investment account: accumulating funds for investment opportunities, such as buying a rental house

4. Fun account: saving money for fun (vacations, concerts, etc.)

5. Giving account: saving money so we could continually provide money to needs we saw in our community

At the time, every one of these items seemed impossible. We had no room in our budget, but I believed strongly in the principle of Step and had to find a way to start working toward these things. My original thought was to put a percentage of our income toward each of these categories so that once we were making more money, the amounts being deposited in each of these goal accounts would increase. We started very small and decided that, no matter what, we would put 1% of our income toward these things each month. That equated to roughly $5 in each account at the time.

This is what the *if–then* statement for this scenario looked like:

If [I want to pay off debt, save for my kids, have money to invest, spend money for fun, and give money when needs arise] . . .

Then [I need to start putting money toward each of these goals]

If [I need to start putting money toward each of these goals] . . .

Then [I need to determine an amount to put toward these goals each time I receive money]

If [I need to determine an amount to put toward these goals each time I receive money] . . .

Then [I need to find a percentage that I can feel comfortable with saving when I receive money]

and

Then [I need to determine what to do when I receive money I wasn't expecting]

My grand vision was to open a bank account for each one of these items, but the amount was so small we had to start out using envelopes. I was excited the first time I took five $5 bills and placed one in each envelope. Amy on the other hand thought I was a little crazy.

After all, even if we did this for an entire year we would only have $60 in each one of the envelopes. It wasn't about the amount, though, it was about the principle of taking steps. These were the only steps we knew to take.

As Amy and I started to make more money, we also made an agreement that we wouldn't add any expenses to our life (that we could control, like a new car) until all of our debt was paid off. We would put any extra money toward debt and then ultimately start increasing the overall percentage we were saving for these things each month.

We were able to pay about $10,000 in debt, save $10,000 toward our future child's expenses, and obtain a rental property in a little less than two years after starting this plan.

At the time we had no clue that Amy would get a bonus at the end of the year or that I would end up getting a raise halfway through the year. I'm 100% convinced that if we hadn't started taking these steps we would have found other "needs" for that money when it showed up.

Now Amy and I are able to put roughly 20% of our income toward these goals each month. They've shrunk to four now since we were able to pay off our debt.

Here is a step-by-step guide to walking through this process: Start by creating your *if* statement. Be as clear and detailed as possible. I recommend using a few questions to form your *if* statement:

What: What do I want?

When: When do I want it?

Quantify: Can I quantify it?

For example:

What: I want to pay off my mortgage

When: In five years

Quantify: $150,000 (the amount I owe)

If statement: If [I want to pay off my mortgage ($150,000) in five years] . . .

That is a clear goal and/or proverbial mile that can be broken down into actions you can take today.

Now let's start the process:

If [I want to pay off my mortgage ($150,000) in five years] . . .

Then [I need to pay off $30,000 per year]

Then [I need to pay off $2,500 per month]

Then [I need to pay off $625 per week]

Then [I need to pay off $125 per day, assuming a five-day workweek]

Then [I need to make an extra $16 per hour, assuming eight hours per day, five days a week]

Let's stop for a second. It's important to walk through the entire process and not shortchange it before you've broken it down to the ridiculous. Some people may feel they can break it down all day long, but an extra $150,000 over five years just isn't possible no matter how you look at it. That is the problem . . . you're not allowing yourself to look at the situation in a different way. You're still focusing on the mile and as long as you focus on the mile you'll never see the step.

Let's keep going. What would you need to do in order to make an extra $16 each hour, assuming a 40-hour work week, to pay off your mortgage?

Then [I should look for jobs that pay $16 more per hour]

Then [I should gain the skills to get the job that makes $16 more per hour]

or

Then [I need find a way to sell five things five days a week for $25]

Then [I need to find something I can sell and make $25 profit]

or

Then [I need to make an extra $5 per hour and cut monthly expenses by $1,700]

Then [I need to ask my boss about a plan to make $5 more per hour and cut cable, eating out, etc.]

Hopefully, you're seeing the pattern by now. *Open your mind to what you can do, not what you can't do.* You can't pay off $150,000 in five years if you don't know what you can do today to start.

It may start by using Netflix instead of cable. That's a step toward the goal. Will that alone get you to your goal? No, but it's a step in the right direction. More importantly, it's not a step in the wrong direction.

The reality is that when you put this formula into place you will find steps that you can start to take. The challenge is to take them no matter how small or insignificant they may seem.

If you get stuck trying to find the steps within your mile it's OK to enlist the help of another person. Consider asking a close friend or trusted advisor to walk through the process with you. I find this helps open up our minds to new ways of thinking about breaking down the mile.

You'll find a handful of other examples in Appendix A using this formula along with a study guide to fill in yourself.

Start breaking your mile down now! Yes, it's OK—you have permission to put down the book and get to stepping.

4
WHEN "BLANK" HAPPENS

I love to be motivated. Who doesn't?

All I need is a great motivational story or inspirational talk to get me feeling invigorated and ready to accomplish anything. Those are the days when "everything is clear" and all obstacles seem so small I wonder why I ever paid them any attention. I'll confess that I get this feeling coming out of a good movie.

Even as a grown adult, I walk out of movies pretending I'm the main character. You should see the way my wife looks at me when we walk out of an action movie and I jump off the sidewalk doing some type of ninja kick. OK, so maybe I have a problem—but come on, you know what I'm talking about.

Inspiration is critical for accomplishment. If we aren't inspired, we have no reason to move.

I happen to like Google's definition of inspiration: "The process of being mentally stimulated to do or feel something, especially to do something creative."

When we are young, inspiration can sway us back and forth like the wind. I like to joke that I'm well rounded because when I was a kid I went through a phase for just about everything.

I was a cowboy for a while. I was also a rapper and a skater. Of course, I was an athlete, but I was also a business tycoon, a preacher, a ninja, a Navy SEAL, and on and on. I believe it was in third or fourth grade that I took three different school pictures: one as a cowboy with hat, boots, and duster; then a quick change into my Dallas Cowboys outfit; and then into my rap star attire. Yes, I believed that I could be all of these things. My parents obviously gave me more freedom than most, but I guarantee almost every child is swayed by the same whims.

We want to emulate the "cool" people we see. Though we may not be as fickle or impressionable as kids, adults do the same thing. We just typically hide it better. Think about a time when you met someone who was significantly more successful than you. Did the thought not cross your mind that you wish you could be more like that person? We all dream and have hopes of being more than we are. When we see people who have the illusion of possessing the things we want, we start to the think about being like them.

Inspiration can be a great thing! However, in kids and in adults, it can be short-lived.

Enter a hint of realism:

When we are young, we are transparent about the inspiration we feel. Why wouldn't we be? A few weeks later and we have forgotten about our plans of being like Chuck Norris. We're on to another adventure. It's OK for children to be so open about their dreams, but at some point in life this behavior becomes socially unacceptable.

As we get older, we begin to dismiss the fleeting emotions that could move us back and forth like the wind. We start to understand that even though it would feel amazing to be a superstar we may not have the time, energy, or talent to accomplish it. We start to see the world as it is. We become adults!

We remember how our dreams are crushed by the alarm clock that wakes us every morning to the reality of a job we are forced to do because of life. We know that our dreams are just dreams and to let ourselves think of something better is an open invitation to disappointment. We become closed-minded and guarded to inspiration. Inspiration is for fools, we may say.

Or maybe we still dream. Maybe we still allow inspiration to capture our hearts. Maybe we are that adult who still believes anything is possible. We get inspired and we take action. We start moving in the direction of our dreams. We start accomplishing again. It feels great, but a few weeks later, life hits and we are thrown off course. The inspiration we once felt seems so far away. It's still faintly burning, but not enough to move us beyond whatever reality we are encountering. We let go and move on.

If only we could feel the way we felt when we first heard that speech or read that book . . . If we could see as clearly as we did that evening when this dream was birthed . . . If we could feel that inspiration every day as we are making the decision to step toward or away from the goal in front of us . . . If only life were perfect and there were no interruptions, we could achieve what we dream.

We will not always feel inspired, but there will always be interruptions in our plans.

WE WILL NOT ALWAYS FEEL INSPIRED, BUT THERE WILL ALWAYS BE INTERRUPTIONS IN OUR PLANS.

The baby is sick, a work trip, the yard needs to be mowed. There will always be someone or something that tells us why we can't. It will seem that there are far more reasons to abandon our plan than to continue forward.

Why? Because "blank" happens. And it happens to all of us. "Blank" can be a lot of things and it's different for all of us, but for the sake of this chapter, I want to focus on three "blanks": feelings, people, and life.

When "Feelings" Happen

We are moved by what we feel. We feel in love. We feel inspired. We feel mad. We feel sad. All of these emotions rush into our lives without even a knock at the door, and as quickly as they come, they are gone like a woman in a country song.

This is fine—it's just a part of being human. The trouble comes when we let our feelings drive our actions, since our actions dictate our outcomes. Here's what I mean:

Fact: Actions = Outcomes

Yes, other variables also affect our outcomes, but it's safe to say that our actions play a *huge* role in getting us to wherever we are.

So, if Actions = Outcomes

and

Our Actions = Our Feelings

Then our outcomes would be completely unpredictable because our feelings are just that—unpredictable.

We tend to believe feelings precede movement, but I challenge that point with strong resolve. Feelings or emotions are the result of something. It may be something good or it could be something bad. You may feel affection for someone just from a simple glance across the room or you may feel furious when that same person does something that annoys you. We feel inspired by something a person says or by a burst of energy (sometimes due to Red Bull).

In several marriage courses I've attended, the instructors make a point to note that feelings are the results of our actions. We can change them. If we do not feel love for our spouse, we should tell them we love them and bring flowers home. Act the way we want to feel and those feelings will come because feelings follow action of some type. I'm a big believer in the concept that love is a choice and not a feeling. Yes, you can feel love and that's a great thing. Feeling is a part of love. But we ultimately choose to love whether or not the feeling is there. Once you choose to love, the feelings of love will follow. Whether these feelings come instantly or down the road is not the point. The point is that we have the ability to change and direct these mystical creatures—our feelings.

We can control and change the way we feel by the choices we make. This may not always be easy, but it is possible. I'll give you another example. Have you ever gone to the gym, but dreaded, aka not "felt" like, working out? Or dreaded pitching a new idea to your boss? Maybe you just felt too tired to work on that business plan, but you did it anyway?

WE CAN CONTROL AND CHANGE THE WAY WE FEEL BY THE CHOICES WE MAKE.

Then you finish the workout or the pitch, or you make great progress on the business plan, and you "feel" this sense of accomplishment and purpose. Just minutes earlier it pained you to take a step toward doing any of these activities and now you feel like a million bucks and couldn't imagine yourself trading the time for something else. Take a couple of minutes to think about what just happened . . .

. . . Another minute please.

Isn't that one of the simplest yet most profound revelations? We can change the way we feel about taking the next step by taking the next step! I hope I'm not the only one getting excited here.

My encouragement is to create your feelings instead of letting them move you. Feelings should follow your lead and they will if you keep them in check.

As a salesman, Stan Goss would have failed miserably if he allowed his feelings to dictate whether he talked to another person. One of his mottos was, "One more call." He told me a story about when he was getting started in chemical sales that has stayed with me.

He realized that to make his draw he needed to sell $300 a day worth of chemicals. To do that he needed two to three sales each day. To get those customers, he figured out that he had to talk to 10 people each day. Just think about that. He had seven people each day tell him no! And they weren't always polite. Sometimes they were disgusted that he would even ask. Oh, and it wasn't like 10 people each day were just waiting to talk to him. He had to drive around to businesses and walk in without anyone expecting him. Heck, a lot of the companies had no solicitation policies.

WE CAN CHANGE THE WAY WE FEEL ABOUT TAKING THE NEXT STEP BY TAKING THE NEXT STEP!

He's told me stories about seeing a back gate open at a warehouse and just letting himself in because he knew if he went through the front door they would turn him away.

If my grandfather had let his feelings move him, he would have been stopped in his tracks seven times every day! It sucks to get turned down. In sales it's especially tough because of how some people act. Instead of being moved by the feeling of rejection, he continued until he found a customer. At the end of the day when he had accomplished his goals he felt great! The seven people that turned him down didn't matter because of the three that said yes.

Also be mindful of letting good feelings lead your actions. There's nothing like the elation that comes with hitting our goals, especially if we had to push through negative feelings before we could even take those steps at all. But it's easy to feel that we deserve a break from stepping after a productive run. *I went to the gym four times this week, so I deserve to skip today. I wrote 10 pages yesterday; I'm on such a roll that it won't matter if I take today off.* Of course, we all need downtime. If you're scheduled to take today off, by all means, put your feet up. But don't let the good feelings steer you off track. If Stan landed six sales within his first eight sales calls, he still made sure he talked to 10 people that day. And unless the next day was Sunday, he went back out for another 10 calls.

We will only accomplish our goals if we create our feelings instead of letting them create us.

WE WILL ONLY ACCOMPLISH OUR GOALS IF WE CREATE OUR FEELINGS INSTEAD OF LETTING THEM CREATE US.

When "People" Happen

There is a popular line from the Bible that I believe is worth sharing: "Fearing people is a dangerous trap" (Proverbs 29:25).

Let's zoom out and think about this for a second. How often have you or someone you know allowed another person's beliefs to dictate what you do? I touched on this earlier when talking about what family or parents may have said about you when you were young, but it rings true throughout life. It's common for us to look to other people for a sense of validation.

It starts with our parents. We have a strong desire to earn their approval and then it continues to teachers, friends, coworkers, etc. We even judge ourselves and our abilities based on random interactions with people in restaurants or coffee shops. In our adolescence we are judged by teachers to decide whether or not we are winners or losers. Once we graduate into life after school, we are judged by a manager or boss. Our entire society is built on the approval or disapproval of people. So it's understandable that we would allow people to dictate what we believe we can do or should do, but this is the trap.

If you allow your life to only reach as high as the potentially jaded beliefs of a teacher, boss, parent, or friend you are not likely to reach your potential. These people may have good intentions, but it can be hard for a person who hasn't achieved to believe another person could. We tend to be selfish and fearful of our own limitations. Those fears are projected on the people we have influence with and a damaging cycle is perpetuated. Or maybe that's not even it—maybe you're just being subjected to someone's bad mood. In any case, others don't get to have that power over you.

Allow yourself to dream. Believe you can achieve more than the limitations placed on you by other people no matter how well intentioned they are. Most stories of great success include overcoming what other people have done or said. The classic stories of Michael Jordan being cut from his high school basketball team or Steve Jobs being kicked out of his own company are two great examples. These men persisted to believe in something bigger than the limitations placed on them by others and that made all the difference.

BELIEVE YOU CAN ACHIEVE MORE THAN THE LIMITATIONS PLACED ON YOU BY OTHER PEOPLE NO MATTER HOW WELL INTENTIONED THEY ARE.

Feelings and people are two forces we can overcome. When we put them in their place, they aren't so bad. There is another force worth mentioning. It's that little thing we call life.

When "Life" Happens

Life is a funny and unpredictable thing. If you have spent

more than a couple of years on this great planet you know that's the truth. It doesn't seem to matter how well you plan—there is a chance something unexpected and uncontrollable will happen. My wife and I love to watch those HGTV shows about flipping houses. Without fail there is always some unforeseen problem that comes up during the middle of construction that ends up costing more money. Sometimes I feel like the homeowner in the show. Shouldn't these professionals know what it would cost?

The reality is that we will never be able to predict what life will throw with 100% accuracy. We have to accept this and learn to turn the seemingly inconvenient challenges of life's unpredictability into some of the greatest building blocks and testaments to our story.

This is especially difficult for me. I'm very good at being disciplined. I can plan out my day perfectly and if all things stayed the same I would breeze through life accomplishing everything I wanted to get done. *But* . . . at least one of these things always seems to happen to disrupt my plans:

- A big project forces me to work late

- The baby gets sick and a week seems to disappear

- The car breaks down

I could go on and I bet you could, too. Things happen and that time you set aside for stepping toward your goals vanishes. A week goes by or maybe two and you realize that you have gotten completely off track. We feel discouraged by the lost progress.

These situations can really knock me off course. Writing this book is a step I'm taking. I go to a coffee shop close to my office from 7 a.m. to 8 a.m. twice a week to write. The first month went great and I was making solid progress, but then, life . . . My wife had an extended work trip and I needed to take the baby to daycare on Tuesday and Thursday, but daycare doesn't start until 9 a.m. and my daughter needs quite a bit of attention in the mornings. It is impossible to step away and write while I'm changing diapers and feeding her. What did I do? Honestly, the first week I didn't write at all. I got off track. The second week I swerved. I wrote at night once the baby went to bed. I had to give up watching a favorite TV show and vegging on the couch, but I kept stepping and got back on track.

Another time about two years ago, I had the perfect storm of situations. I had started doing push-ups and sit-ups every morning and evening. It was my way to move toward being in better shape. I started with 50 a day and worked up to 200 a day. A few weeks into doing 200 a day, my elbows started to hurt. I'm typically the sort of person that pushes through pain, but this was too much for me. I had to stop, so I decided to start running again. This went great for a while until I injured my knee and couldn't put any pressure on it. I was determined to lose the extra weight, so I started swimming laps. It was going pretty well until I had to have a minor surgery on my back. COME ON! Couldn't I get a break? I decided to swerve one more time, or as my friend Selah Hirsch says, "Do the tango!" The only other option I could think of was not physical at all. I had to change my diet, and it worked! I started eating better and I hit my goals despite not being able to exercise.

What about when life is just downright mean? A death of someone close to you. A diagnosis of cancer or some other illness that throws everything off course. Maybe you lose your job or your family. It's a bit easier to swerve when something less permanent happens, but can you do the same thing with events that literally shake you to your core?

Yes, you can. Sometimes these situations change the way you look at things. They may even change what is important, or change you. It's important to remember that it's OK if your goals and desires change. These things may change your step. However, they could also give you more resolve to make an impact with the time you have. What that impact is could change, but the principles of how you make that impact won't.

I remember the day my dad found out he had cancer. I got a text from my stepmom telling me what was going on and asking me to call. My dad and I had been working during the past few years to repair our relationship. Though we weren't as close as we had been when I was young, he was still my dad and I loved him.

That same weekend my roommates/business partners and I moved out of our super-cool high-rise apartment building into a very generous couple's house. We had put the last two years of our life and all of our money into ROOV.com, the web startup company I'd mentioned earlier. We had been pursuing our dreams with a decent amount of traction, but the reality that this business may not be a success was just starting to hit us. We were coming to the end of our road. We couldn't afford to pay ourselves or the rent for our apartment/office anymore.

That weekend marked the beginning of one of the toughest few years of my life. We shut down our business and my dad got worse. Though we kept pursuing our business dreams it just seemed like I couldn't get any traction.

I ended up taking a traditional job to pay the bills, but shortly after that, my dad got so sick that I needed to move to Houston to help him out. I had lost all of my money when ROOV shut down, so I was a bit stuck. My dad didn't have any money. Thankfully, I was able to move to Houston while some family in Arkansas supported me. It was humbling in so many ways.

I met my soon-to-be wife the same weekend that I learned about my dad's cancer diagnosis and moved out of my apartment. Meeting Amy was definitely the silver lining. However, I was the unemployed boyfriend who lost all of his money in a failed venture and ended up in a pretty rough mental state trying to take care of his dying dad. It wasn't what I had always pictured for myself. It was a tough time.

I had been pursuing my dreams until this point. All of this at once stopped me in my tracks and rendered me useless for a decent amount of time.

If I'm completely honest there were several very dark moments and I had the opportunity to completely let go of all of my dreams and desires. And for some time I did.

Here's the point. Life threw me some big curves and while they knocked me off my track for longer than a few months, hope was not lost. Maybe my hope was hiding for a time, but it was still there. No matter what life throws at you there will always be a chance for you to get up and keep going.

Let my life and this book be an example of it.

No matter how hard I have tried to make things go perfectly, I find that "blank" always shows up. Feelings, people, and life are just a couple of the "blanks" that try to force our dreams out the door. So, how do we navigate the "blanks" that come our way?

We stay flexible, we reset, and we reprioritize.

Stay Flexible

This is easier for some and harder for others. Flexibility is not one of my core strengths. I like to set a plan and stick to it at all costs. Black and white with no room for gray. However, we have to be flexible. For me, it can be as small as changing the time I write to the evenings in order to take care of my daughter while my wife is out of town. Or it can be as big as changing the time frame on accomplishing a goal.

The challenge is that the first time you learn about a setback is usually in the moment it happens. The only thing we can do to prepare is to maintain a mindset that we will be flexible when the unexpected happens.

Think back to a time when you were given bad news or faced an interruption to your plan. What was your initial reaction? We all react differently to these situations, but we can train ourselves to be flexible by looking for alternate solutions to our plan. That should be your first thought. If it's not, then it should be the second one because you can choose to think this way.

I have a friend who is in the middle of launching a really cool accessories company. Recently, he discovered that another company had a trademark on the name he had picked for his brand. For the sake of his privacy, I'll keep the names out.

Interestingly enough this company has been known to pursue legal action against anyone who tries to use their mark, even if it isn't exactly the same. My friend was convinced that his brand wouldn't infringe on their mark, but he sought legal counsel. His legal counsel told him there was a 50/50 chance based on history that he would be forced to defend his use of the name. While he might win, it could end up costing $50,000 to fight.

He had to choose: Either he could stay flexible and look for an alternate name to keep moving forward; he could give up on his business; or he could keep going as he was and risk being sued. Being sued was out of the question, and though he felt very strongly about the current brand name, he decided to come up with another name. He stayed flexible and is continuing down the path of launching his newly renamed company.

Flexibility is about being willing to rethink your current game plan. We have to adapt. We must keep an open mind. A no doesn't have to mean no and a roadblock doesn't have to be permanent. It may be a detour, but it's not a dead end.

When I stepped away from my life, friends, and career pursuits to spend time helping my dad through his fight with cancer, I felt like I'd hit a dead end. I went from building the latest in technology and traveling the country evangelizing it to being guided by my dad on how to finish one of his construction jobs while he sat in a chair too weak to move.

A NO DOESN'T HAVE TO MEAN NO AND A ROADBLOCK DOESN'T HAVE TO BE PERMANENT. IT MAY BE A DETOUR, BUT IT'S NOT A DEAD END.

The thoughts going through my mind while in that hot house in downtown Houston were less than positive. If I hadn't stepped in to help my dad run his company, he would have had no way to pay his bills. We left the hospital after a major surgery that removed part of his face, and instead of taking him home to rest, we were on the job site. This was not the plan, but it was reality. For those few months every one of my plans was at a standstill. I had to be flexible and flexibility looked like putting my dreams on hold to take care of my dad. That was the decision I made and I have no regrets about it. My dad ultimately passed away not too long after that. At the same time, Amy and I were in the midst of planning our wedding and a move to Arkansas. It was a mentally and physically challenging time.

Getting back on track was a slow and steady process. I literally did it one step at a time. The first step was to simply allow myself to dream and believe again. My experiences during the previous months had exhausted my ability to believe and I needed to get that back first. My step was to start allowing myself to see a picture of who I wanted to be. My dreams around business, writing, and helping nonprofits started to once again swirl in my mind. These dreams led to stepping and now I'm living in the middle of what those dreams portrayed.

Reset

Four months after my dad passed away, Amy and I got married and we moved to Arkansas. Just to give some more context, the previous year and a half had included the passing of my dad, the shutting down of ROOV, the launching a new tech company called Paratweet, a move to Arkansas, and getting married. I'm sure there were a few other things in there, but that's most of it. When Amy and I returned from our honeymoon to the small home we had purchased in Arkansas, we felt like we were at square one. Paratweet made a profit, but not enough for me to take a salary, so I started a new job working in my family's company. I didn't know what compensation was going to look like. I had spent the last four years chasing my dreams and now I was relegated to watching them all dissolve in front of my eyes. What was I doing with my life? Why was I back in Arkansas working for my family? This wasn't the plan, but it was reality. I had to reset. I had to reevaluate what mattered in life. I had a new wife and I couldn't chase my dreams without thinking about the consequences. I had debt and zero cash. I hadn't been in that place before. Our reset took a couple of months. It was part settling into a new life together in a new place and part trying to rationalize what had just happened and what our dreams were going forward. We put everything on the table and started to look at our lives in a new light.

When we reset, we take a step back and reassess our game plan based on our new circumstances. When "blank" happens, our reality changes. When our reality changes, we may have to change with it. You'll be forced to do this when the unexpected happens, but I would challenge you to do it voluntarily at least three to four times a year. In the business world, we technically do this every quarter with quarterly reviews or other types of meetings meant to let us take a step back and evaluate our progress while charting our future. These pulse checks are critical as you navigate your mile. It's important to keep stepping, but it's just as vital to pause so you can determine whether you need to reroute.

There was a three-month period while writing this book that my schedule went bananas. I was on the road almost every week, with back-to-back meetings from morning till night. I was overwhelmed and had to reset. Thankfully I had accountability to help me do this—a powerful asset to stepping that I'll cover in more detail later. I had been walking through the process of writing *Step* with several people. One was an experienced author who would challenge me in the process of writing every few weeks. He asked tough questions and gave challenging advice based on my answers.

We've had several conversations since that time, and he told me that it was obvious I was overwhelmed due to the sheer business of life. He suggested that I shift my focus from finishing the book to journaling, and his advice was perfectly timed. I wasn't in a place to dedicate the time needed to finishing the book; however, I needed to continue to step. Another friend had also encouraged me to journal. He said that journaling would still keep me on the path forward, but would release the pressure of having to finish within a certain time frame. This was freeing to me. It allowed me to relax as my circumstances adjusted while continuing to move in the direction I needed to go. It was a powerful reset.

Sometimes the perspective you get from a reset shows you that you shouldn't change a thing. I remember a story my grandfather told many times. It was a true reset moment. He had taken a large step to retire from the company he was working for as a chemical salesman and start his own chemical company.

It was a big move, but he had started to gain traction in his new company and things were looking up. Then out of nowhere his previous employer decided to sue him, saying that his non-compete agreement as a salesman made it illegal for him to work in the same field for two years.

Let me put this into perspective. My grandfather's company at the time was small potatoes. He went from selling chemicals to operating a small chemical business while raising four children with my grandmother. He was a busy man. He didn't have the time or money for a lawsuit, but he didn't have much of a choice.

He had made a decision to step and those steps were paying off until all of a sudden this big "blank" happened. The "blank" forced him to reevaluate his decision to start his own company. Should he have done this in the first place? Was he making the right decision to fight the lawsuit? Should he put his career on hold until the non-compete was finished?

My grandfather's morning walks in the woods were filled with lots of questions during this season of his life. He was questioning all of his decisions, and he would need to reset in order to determine the way forward. This reset moment would dictate the course of his life over the next few years.

He had a decision to make. He could give in and settle with his former employer, which would mean giving up his business, or he could take the risk and fight based on his belief that the non-compete was actually illegal.

His mind was made up on the morning of the trial and he

walked into a private room with his attorney. The attorney reiterated that he didn't believe they could win, once again urging him to settle. I can only imagine how resolute my grandfather had to have been to look a far more educated person in the face and tell him, "We won't settle! Get in that courtroom and win the damn case." My grandfather is not a swearing man, but that day he sure wasn't letting anyone detour him from what he believed to be right.

That day a precedent was set in the state of Arkansas that allowed a salesman to compete with a former employer. It provided protection for the American dream, not only to my grandfather, but to anyone in the state who would ever find themselves in a similar situation.

Reset. Take the time to step away from your current chaos and evaluate the bigger picture. Sometimes you can do this in the middle of chaos, but I find it much more effective to get away from the noise of life. If you're in a situation that needs a reset, find a way to get away from the madness and clear your mind so you can effectively reset. Close friends and mentors can also provide great advice during this process.

Reset often, even when life hasn't thrown you a curve ball. It's the time to ask yourself whether you're on the right path. For me, it meant changing my step; for my grandfather, it meant sticking his feet in the ground with firm resolve. We'll experience multiple outcomes to our reset in the course of life. There may be a time when a reset means a complete change in direction and an adjustment to your goal. Other times, as in Stan's case, taking the time to reflect will confirm that you are on the right track.

RESET OFTEN, EVEN WHEN LIFE HASN'T THROWN YOU A CURVE BALL. IT'S THE TIME TO ASK YOURSELF WHETHER YOU'RE ON THE RIGHT PATH.

Reprioritize

Staying flexible and taking a reset are keys to handling what "blank" throws at us. These exercises can also lead us to the realization that we may need to reprioritize. When "blank" happens, our priorities may shift.

After Amy and I had taken the time to reset our lives and accept our new reality, we started to prioritize what was important now. In the beginning we needed to pay off debt. That was something hanging over our heads that had to be fixed. My dreams of becoming a great entrepreneur got reprioritized because I wanted to set my family up for financial success in the immediate future. This prioritization meant I needed steady income. I wasn't going to get that through any kind of new venture, so for a bit my entrepreneurial drive had to concede to a consistent paycheck through my family's company. Sure, this was somewhat discouraging at the time, but it would help us build the foundation we needed to take the risk I'm taking now with my dreams of being an author and speaker.

WHAT WE ONCE THOUGHT TO BE THE GUIDING GOAL IN OUR LIVES MAY BE RENDERED INADEQUATE AS WE EXPERIENCE MORE OF LIFE.

I'll be the first person to convince you to stay the course, but I also want to make it clear that reprioritizing can be just that. This is not quitting; it's course correcting based on reality. Our priorities change as we change. What we once thought to be the guiding goal in our lives may be rendered inadequate as we experience more of life. You may know it's time to start reprioritizing if your reasons for moving toward a specific dream or goal no longer seem worthy of the pursuit. This is an exercise is in self-reflection. We have to ask ourselves questions like:

Do my steps still make sense?

Are my goals still correct based on my current reality?

The most difficult part of reprioritizing can be the need to be honest with ourselves. I've found that most of the time I know when my priorities need to shift, but making the decision to shift them can be difficult.

Other times, our reality may change so radically that the things we once valued as most important may become completely obsolete. Life events can change our perspective drastically. The way I valued things before the passing of my mother and father was very different than after.

I haven't mentioned my mother until now, but she was an amazing woman. I learned a lot from her. Her charisma, her entrepreneurship, and her drive to make sure her son had the best life possible no matter what it cost are all traits that I strive to have in my life.

My parents divorced when I was three and my mother raised me on her own. My mother was diagnosed with bipolar disorder at some point in my young life. It's not something that many people knew. In fact, I didn't even know until several years after her passing.

I saw firsthand the challenges of being a single parent. It's one of the reasons I have such a heart for people who find themselves in situations they wish they weren't in. Parents go out of their way for their children. They change their dreams and their plans almost without thought of consequence.

When I was in sixth grade, my mom threw me a big birthday party at the local skating rink. It cost $150, which was a large order for my mother. She didn't have it. We lived with my grandparents for most of my young life because she couldn't afford a place of our own. We were blessed to have our family's help, but my mom was determined to support us on her own.

I found out when I was older that my mom had sold a collection of dolls to pay for my party. My mom didn't do much for herself, but she had grown to love collecting limited edition dolls. I think they were Barbie, but I'm not certain. I do know she loved this collection; it was probably the only thing she had that was "hers." Yet her priority was me and when she found herself in a position of giving me a party or keeping something for herself, she chose me.

Fast-forward a few years. I'm a senior in high school with all types of ambition. I'm mostly rude to my mother because I'm a teenager. It was that phase in life when family is important, but not as important as being cool. I was often embarrassed by my mom's appearance at social functions. I would quickly dismiss her questions with smug answers. Looking back, if I were her, I would have put myself in some form of punishment much more than she did!

My priorities at the time were all about myself. I would say that's pretty natural for a teenager.

Then, the worst night of my life happened. I came home late one Tuesday evening to find a note from my mother on the entrance to our home. It read, "Son, please call the doctor or your family. I've shot myself and I don't want you to see me like this."

That night everything changed in my life. It's been over 10 years, but I can still feel the pain of that night as I'm writing these words. The following minutes, hours, weeks, and months altered my life dramatically. "Blank" struck in a way I could have never imagined.

Things that seemed immensely important before that night—like what my friends thought of the car I drove or the clothes I wore—were immediately gone. An overwhelming compassion and emphasis on family and relationships came over me. A desire to help people suffering like my mother was born. I had always been compassionate, but this ignited something new in me.

In the weeks and months that would follow my mother's death, I had a reprioritization around family. I moved things in my schedule to make time for family and friends. I also forever changed the way I say goodbye, not taking for granted that I would see them again, but embracing the moments I have. I became more aware of those around me and did my best to be aware of their struggle so I could help in any way possible.

Since I was young, I have dreamed of creating a fund or endowment for the purpose of sustainable giving to provide money for those in need, but I haven't made any large strides toward it until this year. My dreams around being a successful businessman and providing well for my future family didn't go away; however, my philanthropic dreams demanded a place of priority in my steps.

The point in all of this is that it's OK to change course if that change of course is needed. When you find yourself in "blank" happening, just take a step back. Be flexible, reset, and if needed reprioritize. This doesn't mean you stop stepping, it just means your step may change or things you're stepping for may adjust.

I've never regretted continuing to step, but I have time and again regretted my decision to allow my step to be stopped.

5
THE ANTIDOTE

What is your reason for stepping? Perhaps you want a better life for your family, to change your financial circumstances, or to improve your quality of life by becoming healthier. It could be to become a great role model for your children or to become the next CEO of your organization.

Whatever your reason for stepping, you won't get far if you let yourself lose sight of it.

We step because we want to get somewhere we are not. But when our step becomes hard we tend to forget the big picture and start to fixate on the pain in the moment. The lure of giving up can be so strong and sweet if we don't shift our focus back to the big win.

We can't escape the temptation to give up, but we *can* arm ourselves with an antidote when the easy road beckons us to stop stepping. That antidote is perspective.

I love Dictionary.com's definition of antidote: "Something that prevents or counteracts injurious or unwanted effects."

Our "unwanted effect" in this case is failing to achieve our dream, and the antidote is perspective on what the future can be. When we have a constant vision of where we want to be and we've broken down the path into bite-size steps, we are insulating ourselves from giving up. Giving up is that "thing" that will cause us to get the exact opposite of what we want.

Let's say your goal is to run a marathon. Your steps may include eating healthy and running a few times a week. The steps are attainable and believable, but your motivation is that larger vision of getting healthier and setting a great example for your kids that you can do anything you set your mind to. We must attach our steps to our *reason for stepping* and keep that in the forefront of our minds.

There is a big difference between looking at the mile and looking at the reason. The mile is what it takes to achieve your goal. It's the work, the sweat, and the pain. The goal is the "why" behind the mile. It's the thing that drives you to step. The goal is your chance to dream, and to let your dreams take you places. My dream vacation involves staying in a hut (it's a nice hut) in the Maldives that's built on top of crystal blue water. Sometimes I'll Google pictures of resorts on the water in the Maldives. The beautiful pictures instantly take me there and I can see myself waking up to breakfast in bed and then hopping into my "private" ocean for a morning swim! It's going to be amazing. This is thinking about the reason why I'm taking the steps to save for this trip.

Now, let's say I switch from looking at pictures of this beautiful resort to looking at the price tag. I start to think about the $1,000 per night hut rental + food + airfare. Then I think about the fact that I would want to stay more than just a few days so I'm suddenly looking at $20,000 for the trip. Now let's say my original travel budget for the year was $5,000. When Amy and I set out to achieve this goal we knew we'd have to budget more funds toward travel, so we cut spending in other areas. It means less eating out, a tighter grocery budget, and no room for spending beyond the essentials. It's doable, but it can be a real pain when Amy and I are itching to pick up Friday night sushi after a long week, or when the newest iPhone beckons me to upgrade. In those moments, we wield our antidote. We will ourselves to think of the goal—the reason we're taking these steps—and our perspective shoots right back into focus. Take-out dinner and shiny gadgets don't sound as sweet as morning dips in our private ocean.

Take Daydreaming to the Next Level

Here's an exercise that might help if you're struggle to separate the mile from the goal. Find a quiet place where you won't be disturbed. Maybe it's in your car parked outside of your office or a park close to your house. Set your phone to "do not disturb" and set the timer for 15 minutes. Then write down what it feels like to be at your destination—the end of your mile.

When dreaming about my vacation to the Maldives, I might write things like this:

I'm waking up to the sound of a cool breeze.

I'm walking five steps from my bed to cannonball into the crystal blue ocean.

I'm watching the sunset with my wife in a hammock over the water.

I don't have a care in my mind.

I'm starting to think of moving to the Maldives.

When dreaming about completing that marathon, your list might look something like this:

I'm crossing the finish line as my husband and kids are cheering from the sidelines.

Now that I'm in excellent shape I can carry my toddler in the hiking backpack as our family goes on nature walks, and we can go on more adventurous trails.

My older kids are seeing their mom set a difficult goal and achieve it, and they know they can do the same.

Once you have done this for a solid 15 minutes, you should have a list that describes what it will be like to find yourself at the end of your mile. Remember, this exercise has nothing to do with how you get there. It's all about being there. It's fun!

Now keep this list with you. Any time you start to lose motivation, pull it out and take five minutes to remember why you're stepping into your mile. You might just feel the antidote zap through you as it melts away any thoughts of giving up.

Remember Your Why

Asking "why" is a powerful tool in gaining perspective. At Oven Bits, the software company that I'm a part of, this is a crucial exercise that we bake into all of our work. Every week at our company meeting someone gets up and talks about the "why" behind a current or recent project. This week a developer read a question that was posted on an application that we built in conjunction with the National Breast Cancer Foundation:

"Should I tell my 10-year old-daughter that I've been

diagnosed with breast cancer?"

Then he read three answers from mothers who had told their young children about being diagnosed and gave the woman great advice and encouragement.

It's easy for us to get so focused on the design and code that we forget the "why" behind our work. This small reminder and ones like it bring a sense of purpose and drive to the lines of code and Photoshop files that can feel tedious.

The same thing will be true in your life. At some point, the step will seem monotonous. Your reason for stepping may be as impactful, or more impactful, than the examples I've shared, but when you lose sight of it, it's as if it was never there. I would encourage all of us to ask ourselves "why" every time we step, especially when we find ourselves questioning whether we should step at all.

Stan took a big risk when he moved from working for an established company to starting his first business. The risk became even more real when that established company sued him for it. The lawsuit went on for months and weighed on him every day as he was trying to run and grow a new company. He was up early each morning and spent quite a bit of time away from home. Did the thought of returning back to work at an established company cross his mind? Of course it did. He was in the middle of a struggle and it would have been easy to lose his perspective, but he was driven by a bigger goal. He had a vision to create a place where his kids could always have a job if they wanted one. He didn't want them to ever have to worry about finding work and struggle the way he did. He wanted to provide an opportunity for his kids to have something he never did. He held on to this vision during the tough times and it carried him through. Not only did he accomplish that vision for his kids, but it has provided the same opportunities for many of his grandchildren.

I've committed to writing twice a week in the early mornings before work. At some point I may lose focus on why I'm getting up so early and my motivation for writing could wane. In fact, just this morning I woke up and thought about how I need a little bit more sleep and almost went back to bed . . . but then I told myself no. My dream is too big. There are people whose futures depend on my small sacrifice of waking up early. I have a goal to help people achieve their goals. I have a desire to walk into Barnes & Noble one day and see my book sitting on the bestseller shelf. This dream is what drives me to keep stepping when the steps get harder.

Create a Vision Board

Another great way to remember your goal is to literally put it in front of you with a vision board. A vision board is a collage of pictures and phrases that capture your dreams. Think

Pinterest . . . for your dreams. Visions boards are great for a jolt of inspiration, but I suggest taking yours off the screen and into your practical life. It can be as detailed or simple as you want, as long as it reminds you why you step. Put your vision board somewhere you will be forced to see it every day. My wife and I recently wrote our big dreams on our bathroom mirror with dry-erase markers. We see it every morning when we are getting ready. When I was young, I kept a picture in my wallet of the car I wanted. I saw it every time I opened my wallet and it was a constant reminder of why I was working hard to save money.

Keeping the vision clear in front of you can be difficult at times. We all get busy, and though we have a picture on our mirror or a vision board on our refrigerator, we might find ourselves looking at it, but not actually taking notice. My advice is to schedule consistent time to look at and think about your vision. This may mean Googling images of the Maldives or spending five minutes before everyone gets up looking at your vision board and imagining yourself there. Combining a clear vision of your goal with steps for consistent incremental progress is a powerful way to keep you energized as you walk toward your dreams.

Talk About It

Simply talking about your vision can be a major motivator. It doesn't matter whether you're talking to your spouse, a good friend, a business partner, or someone else. It's the exercise of talking about where you will be one day that can be extremely powerful in maintaining perspective. As part of my plan to market this book, I'm talking to people every day about the vision. It's not easy because I'm working a more than full-time job; however, I've made it a consistent practice. Every time I talk about it, I find a shot of energy and motivation soon follows. It also typically yields a few steps. For instance, the extra boost of energy that comes after talking to someone moves me to write another blog post or talk to someone else.

Make it a point to communicate your vision and you will find the vision stays clearly in front of you.

Chase & Cambryn's Big Vision: Living Debt Free

I want to introduce my dear friends Chase and Cambryn Willsey. My wife has been friends with Cambryn since the fourth grade. Chase and I met several years back and we hit it off the first time we met. Chase and Cambryn introduced me to my wife. Needless to say, we know each other well.

The Willseys had a fairly substantial amount debt when they got married and continued to amass more due to certain life events. It was a combination of school loans, hospital bills, and other various things. I remember the day they made a decision to be debt free. They had a resolve. They knew that getting out of debt was a key to providing the future they wanted to give their children.

For Chase and Cambryn, getting out of debt was about changing their family's financial trajectory. Chase's family tree was made up of financial struggles. Everyone in his family had struggled and this really hit him when his grandparents passed away. He was newly married at the time and was thinking how much of a difference even a small inheritance would have made in his family's life. He decided that this was something he wanted to provide not only to his children, but to their children as well.

He wanted to change a negative legacy in his family, and the key to that was getting out of debt.

Chase and Cambryn knew exactly what they wanted, but getting it was a completely different story. They made the commitment to start making small changes in their life.

One of their many steps was cutting cable. That's about $100 a month, and compared to their debt, it seemed pretty small, but it was a step. They went without cable for over three years. They did numerous other small things like planning meals and using cloth diapers with their first child. All of these things added up and they started paying down debt.

When Chase got a promotion, they didn't add cable back or change any of their small steps. They continued to plug away. They had a vision of being debt free and they kept that at the forefront of their minds.

Another step they took was selling Chase's dream truck. It was a 1995 Land Cruiser and for an outdoorsman like Chase this was *the* truck! This beautiful vehicle was a project, though. There was quite a bit of work to do even though it was fit to drive on a daily basis. The other factor was the cost of gas. The 1995 Land Cruiser was far from a hybrid—it was the ultimate gas guzzler.

Selling the Land Cruiser provided enough money to pay off Cambryn's car loan and let Chase buy a less expensive and more fuel efficient car for his daily commute. This one step was pretty impactful. Not only were they able to have two paid-off cars (one less monthly payment), but they were also able to save a few hundred bucks a month in gas.

Chase doesn't feel he gave up his dream car forever. One day he plans to have a Land Cruiser again, but for now this step was monumental in helping his family break a pattern of being in debt for as long as he had been alive. "Living the dream of being debt free was more important than owning my dream vehicle," he said.

Another step the Willseys took was to have Cambryn continue working until their second daughter was born instead of staying home from the time they had their first. They both dreamed of having Cambryn stay at home with their daughters, but for now, they organized their finances in a way that allowed them to live off Chase's salary so they could use Cambryn's to pay down debt. Cambryn continued to work until their debt was paid off. It just happened to coincide with the birth of their second daughter, which was a nice surprise. Now she's able to stay home with both children as they have always wanted, but it required three years of sacrifice.

It took Chase and Cambryn over three years to pay off their debt, which is pretty cool when you think about it since a lot of people in that situation could spend 20 years or more to do the same. They have changed the course of their family's life forever. We went on a trip together not long after they paid their last bill and I can't tell you how excited they were.

My friends had a very clear picture of the near- and long-term effects of their decisions to step. These goals were in the front of their mind every day as they took the steps necessary to achieve debt freedom. If they had lost this vision, their story could have turned out quite a bit differently. In fact, in Chapter 13, "When You Don't Step," I'll take you down the alternate path the Willseys could have experienced.

Why We Lose Perspective

How can we get so far off track when we have such life-altering goals in mind? You'd think that once we know the power of a step and the future that it will produce we would never stop stepping. Well, the act of taking small steps is simple, but it can be hard to maintain the perspective that keeps us moving. We constantly face the temptation to give up, and this is normal. I believe there are four main reasons we lose our perspective. It's time to expose them so that you can have a better chance at defeating them when they come.

1. Comfort

When we view comfort as more valuable than our reason for stepping, we have lost perspective.

Chase and Cambryn could have decided at any moment to turn their cable back on. They may have reasoned that it's really not that much money every month, and after all, shouldn't they still enjoy life? This attitude is common in the middle of pursuing a major achievement. It's the attitude of "momentary self-preservation." In the moment, we decide that a small amount of comfort is worth more than reaching our desired outcomes.

Of course, when we have perspective, it's obvious that the benefits of our larger goals—like living debt free or having ultimate health—outweigh any little comforts that may come with, say, having cable or sleeping in. When compared side by side, the steps nearly always seem insignificant to the culmination of what those steps can produce. The challenge is that in the moment when things feel hard we're not thinking clearly enough to do these actions-versus-results comparisons. Instead we allow emotions and the desire for some additional comfort to override our dreams.

HOWEVER, WE STRUGGLE TO DECIPHER MOMENTARY COMFORT FROM LASTING COMFORT.

Don't get me wrong—comfort in and of itself is not a bad thing. There's nothing I want more than to be comfortable. I have a nice bed and a pretty comfy couch. Come to think of it, most of my life is based on being as comfortable as possible. And in this lies the challenge. We ultimately desire comfort and when comfort shows itself to us we run toward it. *However, we struggle to decipher momentary comfort from lasting comfort.*

We're naturally motivated to make decisions based on comfort. Many of our dreams represent comfort in some form when you get to the heart of them. Whether it's being comfortable with the way you live your life, being comfortable with your body, being comfortable with the legacy you leave for your family, or being comfortable with the house you live in, we strive for comfort, so it only makes sense that we would be drawn to it. But be careful not to let momentary comforts pull you away from the true comforts you desire, which lie in accomplishing your dreams.

I believe momentary comfort is the reason most people never succeed. There are other factors, of course, but think about it: The only reason I wouldn't get up to write my book is because I want a little more comfort. I want some more sleep. The only reason the Willseys would have kept cable is because of comfort. They want to relax on the sofa and watch ESPN. The only reason my grandfather would have stopped knocking on doors would have been for comfort. He was cold and tired and wanted to go home.

Comfort sets a trap for us. It whispers in our head the wrong thoughts that feel right in the moment but in the long term could be detrimental. Yes, the couch will provide momentary comfort . . . But it may also provide lifelong regret.

Being comfortable with their financial situation and the legacy they leave for their children is more important to Chase and Cambryn than sitting on the couch after a long day. Being comfortable with the message I put out in the world through this book is more important than an extra hour in bed, even on mornings when I'm rolling on just a few hours' sleep. We all struggle with this. I forget about the dream and sink into the "need" for some momentary comfort.

> ## 66

A step not taken is a step in the wrong direction, and a step further from the person you want to be.

CHRISCAPEHART.CO

Snap it, remember it, share it.

#STEPBOOK

What does this statement mean to you?
Write it down.

_____

_____

_____

_____

CHRISCAPEHART.CO

Think about it, wrestle with it, do it.
#STEPBOOK

Chase and Cambryn didn't succumb to reactivating their cable until they were out of debt, but they fought the temptation on a regular basis.

When we find ourselves in these moments, we should think about where we are in comparison to where we want to be. That will make us uncomfortable in the most comfortable setting.

While momentary relief may not seem all that bad the stakes are usually bigger than missing one day. A step not taken is a step in the wrong direction, and a step further from the person you want to be. We are always moving in one direction or another. We are building toward momentum in a positive or negative direction. Each small decision makes a difference.

Keep the end game in mind. And for those times when everything inside of you is telling you to give up—remember the "why" behind your step and let that motivate you to make the right choice. Your dream of a better life is worth the small amount of comfort you may give up to be the person you were meant to be.

2. Size

If the perceived value of the thing you want is not big enough to make you move, you probably won't—at least not for long.

We have to strive for something that is bigger than the pull to give up. Our goals should be ambitious. They should make a difference in our lives and in the lives of others. If the "thing" you are going after doesn't make you move, if it's not worth getting out of bed for, then you won't. It's simple. If the benefit we receive from the work we do is less than the effort it takes to achieve—we will give up.

IF THE "THING" YOU ARE GOING AFTER DOESN'T MAKE YOU MOVE, IF IT'S NOT WORTH GETTING OUT OF BED FOR, THEN YOU WON'T.

Let's take a basic example. Though most would rather sleep in every day they will choose to wake up and go to work. Why? It's typically not out of a loving desire for sacrifice. It's because the benefit of being able to pay one's bills and have food on the table outweigh the cost of waking up.

Remember, we are typically driven by comfort. Were it not for something we desire more than we desire our immediate comfort, we would always opt for comfort today.

Perspective plays a big role in the size problem. You probably are chasing something big, but the drudgery of your mile can make you forget how much your goal means to you and to others. Maybe you haven't stopped recently enough to truly think about what starting that nonprofit, losing that weight, or getting out of debt would do for those around you.

My dream of creating a fund for the purpose of sustainable

giving is actually a driving force behind the way I live. I want to help people who are struggling and my personal belief system tells me that this is a bigger goal than anything else I could wish to accomplish. Yet I've let a considerable amount of time pass without taking the action I'm encouraging in this book.

Why? It's because I let the impact of this dream slip from my mind. I would think about the idea often, but it's not until Mother's Day at my local church that it hits me. I see a single mom sitting in a seat in front of me, I see the love she has for her kids—I saw it in my own mother—and I'm filled with an overwhelming sense of compassion to help her in some way. It's in these moments that the dream of my fund comes rushing back and I find a reignited passion for what might be the largest goal I will ever accomplish.

I have to keep the people I want to help in the forefront of my mind. I have to keep the vision clear. When I think about my dream in financial terms only, it loses its power to drive me. But when I think about the people I could help, I find myself driven with a power that I didn't realize I had.

We need to maintain our perspective so we can remember just how big our goal really is. If we're worried we'll lose sight of our vision, the tools in this chapter can help. In my case, I should keep the stories of families I haven't been able to help in front of me every day. Maybe this is a vision board or maybe it's talking to local nonprofits about how I might be able to help the single parents in our community. Whatever I do, I have to keep the reason in clear view or else my goal will start to appear smaller than it actually is.

Your vision is probably worth the cost, but ultimately, you have to decide for yourself what's worth it and what's not. *If you don't believe it's worth it, don't expect yourself to achieve it.* However, if you say you believe your desire is worth the sacrifice and you still fail to move or move consistently, you have to question your sincerity.

3. Magic

We all want magic to take over . . . and sometimes we believe it will. If you're counting on magic, you've lost your perspective.

Why do we put so much credence on illusions? Our society has been rendered speechless time and time again by "magic." However, if any magician is honest, they'll tell you that there is really no such thing as magic. I know that a magician would never admit it, but there is always an explanation to the trick that seems unexplainable. The older we get, the more we realize magic is just that . . .

However, most of us wouldn't mind a little magic in our lives. It would be great to miraculously achieve the thing we set out to accomplish without having to deal with the necessary steps to get there.

Or maybe you're not counting on magic to make your life easier, but how about luck? I love the definition of "luck" found in Webster's Dictionary: "A purposeless, unpredictable, and uncontrollable force that shapes events favorably or unfavorably for an individual, group, or cause."

Luck is purposeless, unpredictable, and uncontrollable. Yet, we in the United States spent about $70 billion on the lottery in 2015. That doesn't even include casinos. Hey, I'm not throwing stones. I'll be the first to admit I love a scratch-off ticket, but no way will I bet my future on it.

The lottery, luck, and the like give us the chance to bypass normal means of acquiring something we want—in most cases, wealth. It would be nice to bypass the long process for becoming the person we want to be or achieving the thing we want to achieve. Who doesn't like the FastPass at Disney World?

If you're reading this book, there's a pretty solid chance that you don't believe magic or luck will get you where you want to go. But here's the catch: Sometimes we rely on "magic" without even knowing it.

We've talked about the power of belief and how we can actually change our thinking through what we say. We've also talked about imagining ourselves at the end of our goal and thinking about our "why" to maintain perspective. These are all necessary, but without the action to follow them up, it's as if we're hoping for magic to take over.

If we say we can do it, believe we can do it, and even look at our vision board every day but never do it, then we've fallen into the trap of magical thinking.

Magic also likes to wear a common disguise: It's called procrastination. If you keep telling yourself you can definitely run that 5K, create that business plan, or write that next chapter, but just not today, you're in the trap.

Are you doing as much as you're thinking about doing? Wishing something into existence is not a good strategy. It's easy for us to get distracted in only thinking about our dream. If you find yourself relying more on a hope and a prayer than on the action you are taking, it's time to shift back into gear and take the steps in front of you.

It's time to kick magic in the butt and put it on the line. We know it's worth it. We've spent most of this chapter talking about that. The magic formula for kicking magic in the butt is simple: *Do something.*

Here are some signs you are letting magic get the best of you:

- Your friends keep asking you about your dream to start a coffee shop and your answer is, "I'm still thinking through the right approach," or "I'm still waiting on the right timing."

- You ask your boss why you keep getting passed over for a promotion and he says something to the effect of, "You haven't done anything different."

- You find yourself wishing your dreams would come true sooner, but spend two hours every night in front of the TV instead of chasing your dream.

Please don't fall into the trap of thinking that magic or luck will get you anywhere. It is that belief that may stop you from doing the non-magical things it actually takes to achieve your goals.

How do you change your belief in magic? You do something. That's the entire point of this book.

Look, I'm not saying that something extraordinary may not happen to you, but you cannot count on it. Counting on magic or luck is preparing to be disappointed. Just look at the odds on the back of any lottery ticket.

4. Belief

You've lost your perspective if you still don't really believe you can accomplish what you've set out to do.

As mentioned earlier, belief is critical to accomplishing anything. That's why it's one of the first things covered in this book. However, the point of Step is getting you to see the logical process involved in accomplishment. You may not initially believe that you can accomplish something or be the person you want to be, but if you can believe in taking a step and see how that step can lead to accomplishment . . . then you have a shot.

EVERY MILE HAS A CERTAIN NUMBER OF STEPS, AND WHEN YOU IDENTIFY THOSE STEPS, YOU CAN IDENTIFY THE PATH TO BELIEVING.

When you are struggling with belief, you are most likely struggling with perspective. Every mile has a certain number of steps, and when you identify those steps, you can identify the path to believing.

When we don't believe we can accomplish, then our perspective has shifted in the wrong direction. The enormity of our mile is paralyzing, and it can make it difficult to keep going.

If you're struggling with belief, you need to rebuild it by focusing on what you believe you can do. In this case, forget the mile, and even the larger goal, for a brief time. Just look at the steps in front of you. If you don't believe you can conquer the steps, break them into even smaller steps.

So if you don't believe you can write a whole business plan for your coffee shop, forget the whole plan. Just look at the individual sections: the executive summary, sales and marketing, products and services, budget projections, etc.

If you don't believe you can write a single section, break those sections into smaller sections. Just write a list of your products and services. Now write one sentence describing each item. Now price out each item. Keep breaking it down until you believe you can do the small thing. Then keep going. This will rebuild your momentum, and soon enough, you'll start to believe again.

Keeping your perspective is a challenge worth contending with. It's our best defense against the pull to give up, whether we're struggling to believe in ourselves or we let smaller distractions like comfort get in the way of our dreams. The tools in this chapter will help you regain perspective if you're struggling to keep on. But how you approach keeping your vision in front of you is not what matters. It's that you do it.

6
MOMENTUM

Momentum is a force that makes each new step more powerful than the one that came before it. It's that sweet spot you reach after a long period of sweat just to get off the ground. In business this may look like the point at which each new client is no longer just paying for overhead, but bringing in profit. The profitability of that next customer is so much higher than the ones that preceded it. Momentum can be described many ways, but the results are the same every time. *It's the moment when effort starts to produce results at a multiplied rate of return.*

I'd go as far as saying that momentum is the holy grail of progress. It's an amazing place to be and it's tempting to look for shortcuts to get there. Or worse, we can fool ourselves into thinking of momentum as magic; that it's something that just happens if we're lucky.

SOON ENOUGH OUR EFFORTS LITERALLY CREATE A FORCE THAT IS STRONGER THAN ANY ONE STEP COULD GENERATE ON ITS OWN.

Momentum is the byproduct of action. In this book, we break down action into small, achievable steps. You won't catch momentum unless you keep stepping. It's that simple. One step builds on the next, which builds on the next, and so on. Soon enough our efforts literally create a force that is stronger than any one step could generate on its own.

There is a great example I've been hearing since I was young: How much money would you have if you doubled a penny every day for 30 days? If you haven't heard this story before, take a guess.

Any thoughts? Twenty bucks, $50, or even $100?

If you were to double a penny every day for only 30 days, you would have over $10 million at the end of 30 days. This illustration is typically used to describe compounding interest and time value of money. These concepts are used by financial planners to show people how investing a little now (consistently) can be worth a large amount in the future. Dave Ramsey used a similar illustration when I saw him speak to show how paying cash for your car and investing what you would have paid in interest in a good mutual fund would leave you with several million dollars at the end of 30 or 40 years. It's funny how that could be the difference in being able to retire or not.

These examples are convincing because we can clearly calculate the results, but the same principles apply to anything you are stepping toward. This is why I'm so passionate about convincing people to start, and start with something they can keep doing over time.

As you take steps, those steps start to give you momentum toward your goal. Once you have started to achieve momentum, the step you took yesterday is a bit easier to take today. In fact, it may be just as easy to take two steps today as it was to take one yesterday. As you start to feel momentum, you start to add more energy and increase the number of your steps.

I mentioned this concept earlier when talking about working out. If you do a 15-minute workout for 30 days, you will have more energy on the 31st day than you had when you started. The consistency has built your strength and stamina. Now 30 minutes may be just as easy as 15 were before. Also, you have created a habit. You now feel a sense of accomplishment and that drives you to want to do more. You have mastered that first step and now you want to take bigger steps.

This is psychological, it is physical, and it is mathematical. There is an increase in our desire, ability, and drive to step when we've been stepping.

I hope we can all reach momentum. It's that point as a salesman when all of your consistency in cold-calling and emailing leads starts to pay off at a multiple. It's when you used to close one account for every 100 you talked to and now you close two because there is such a backlog of people with whom you have communicated and time brings some of them around. It happens because after a year of stepping, the 25 customers you signed refer 25 more on top of the 25 new ones you will close this year. This is exactly what happened to my grandfather when he started out in sales.

Stan worked to build momentum selling cookware while still maintaining his full-time job in the Army for more than three years. Day after day, he took steps after work to put his family in the financial position he had always desired. He was making more money with his after-work steps than at his full-time job. When the time came to reenlist in the Army, Stan had a choice to make. Because of the momentum he had built over the last three-plus years of stepping, he was able to confidently forgo the opportunity to reenlist in the Army and begin selling cookware full-time. He had been working days and nights for over three years to get himself into a financial position to be able to do something like this and now it was a reality. It's pretty interesting to think about how impactful steps can be in this context. In the grand scheme of things, stepping for three years pales in comparison to the 50-plus years of business success that followed hitting momentum.

Stan continued to leverage momentum for decades after leaving the Army. After selling his chemical business and retiring for a few years, he decided to start a vitamin company. I think the main reason behind this was that he and my grandmother had been taking vitamins from another company and he didn't like the customer service. OK, and he may have been getting a little bored in retirement. He invested $10,000 to get it started. Not much when you consider he had recently sold a company for a few million.

Did he hire anyone? No. This multimillionaire went back to his roots knocking on doors. This time around, he started striking up deals with local businesses to sell his vitamins in their stores. It was slow and steady, but a couple of years in, he had built what I would call some momentum. The company was doing about $50,000 a month in sales through several hundred salespeople working on commission. This may sound like a lot of money, but remember there is overhead, employees, etc.

It was enough to keep him busy and allowed him to hire one or two of his kids. My mom was one of his first employees in the new venture. I was in second grade at the time and "home schooling." I put that in quotes because I was actually at the office with my mom and grandfather every day. And instead of schoolwork, I was helping pack the bottles with vitamins. Don't worry, I had supervision. I was paid a penny for every bottle I filled. Come to think of it, I feel like I may have been getting ripped off.

For three years, my grandfather had steadily worked to create this opportunity for our family and we were all pretty happy. Then, one day, momentum hit. A man came to my family from Oklahoma and said he had an idea that could help our company grow at a fairly staggering rate. I remember watching them discuss and draw on napkins. The idea came in the form of an adjustment to the way the salespeople were compensated. The man proposed that we give our salespeople, the majority of whom were part-time, a larger commission sooner. This would motivate them to sell more than they already were.

Within a day my grandfather had made the decision to give it a try. The steps he had taken over the last year gave him the infrastructure and ability to make that decision. Three years earlier that would have never even been a possibility.

Then as if out of nowhere the company started to grow. The first month after this change in compensation for the sales team, the company did over $250,000 in business. Yes, it went from $50,000 to $250,000 in 30 days. Crazy!

On the outside, it looked like this happened overnight, but we all knew it had been building for three years. All of Stan's previous work intersected with this new opportunity, which allowed him to amplify his efforts. That's how momentum works and you never know when it will propel you to a level you never thought possible.

It's that point when you are eating more healthy food every day than not and it's easy. Momentum is the wings that help put a lift in our efforts. You can reach momentum and continue to build momentum as you continue to step.

Jim Collins's book *Good to Great* talks about the flywheel concept. He explains how good businesses don't become great overnight or because of one major event. It is not a big bang, but a cumulative process that takes consistent effort over time. He compares achieving greatness in business to turning a large metal flywheel. After struggle and effort, you are able to slowly turn the flywheel one full turn, but you don't stop. You keep pushing until you have gone around twice. Then, it starts to get a little bit easier as you go around the third and the fourth time. However, you have never stopped pushing. Finally you reach a point of momentum where the flywheel is actually turning on its own. This is the moment of momentum. Jim goes on to tell a story about a company he studied while writing the book. He said that from the outside they could pinpoint the moment that the company took off down to the exact day. It was obvious. Yet when talking to the CEO, the best he could do was point to a nine-year period of time.

From the outside, it typically seems as if there is one major event that catapults a company or person into the spotlight of their desires. The truth is that this moment of momentum was being developed with consistent movement over a long period of time.

FROM THE OUTSIDE, IT TYPICALLY SEEMS AS IF THERE IS ONE MAJOR EVENT THAT CATAPULTS A COMPANY OR PERSON INTO THE SPOTLIGHT OF THEIR DESIRES. THE TRUTH IS THAT THIS MOMENT OF MOMENTUM WAS BEING DEVELOPED WITH CONSISTENT MOVEMENT OVER A LONG PERIOD OF TIME.

If you've ever taught a child how to ride a bike, or if you remember learning to ride a bike, you have seen this principle work. In fact, every time you ride a bike, you take the necessary steps to gain momentum. Think about it. The first time you push the pedals, the bike is a bit wobbly and the pedals sometimes feel like they are stuck in the mud. That first rotation of the pedals isn't always easy. However, with each pedal it gets a bit easier and then the bike stabilizes (almost like magic). If you pedal long enough, you build so much momentum that you can stop pedaling, put your hands in the air, and coast on the work you have accomplished.

Just like the first pedals were wobbly and hard, the first steps can sometimes seem that way, but if you keep moving forward, you will find yourself where you dream of being. Please push through because there is nothing quite as special as being able to put your hands in the air and let the momentum of your steps carry you beyond your own strength.

Don't Stop Once You Get There

What you do once you've reached momentum is just as important as getting to momentum. The natural tendency when you reach momentum is to coast, like I mentioned above. You take your hands off the handlebars, stop pedaling, and finally take a deep breath. Even though you still haven't reached your ultimate goal, you are now in a place where you can see the finish line and feel victory on the horizon. You might start to believe that victory is inevitable. This is great! I want us to feel this way, *but* don't smell the roses for too long, or you might find yourself picking thorns out later.

The worst thing you could do at this point is let off the gas or stop pedaling and lose the momentum you worked so hard to gain. I've seen it happen too often. We get comfortable and lazy because we know that we have the wind at our back. We don't have to pedal quite as hard to go the same speed, so we don't. Please don't fall into this trap. When you have reached momentum, you should not slow your step. It would be better to push even harder, but at the very least you should maintain the pace. Getting to momentum is a challenge and it can be pretty defeating to lose the momentum once you have achieved it.

I'm currently the CMO at a software company called Oven Bits. At the time of this writing, Oven Bits has been around for almost five years. The founders started the company from nothing and have slowly and steadily been building it over the past few years. There were times when they didn't even take a salary just to keep things moving. The first few years were a true grind. Everyone in the company did everything. The founders were also the top designers and developers. The company was growing at a healthy rate every year. We had been producing great work that was being featured by Apple and Google. One of the apps we produced hit #1 in the iTunes store. All of these things were starting to create momentum and growth for the company. It was about three years in when I joined to focus on business development. The executive team described to me how there had never been a true effort to grow the company's business. They had been so focused on producing the work that came in that there wasn't time to focus on developing new business. Honestly, that's a great problem to have and speaks to the type of work the guys were producing. However, to truly scale you need a focus on developing new business at all times—and the right type of business.

I joined in 2013 with this goal in mind. We wanted to grow our services business while developing new software channels and scaling the business's revenue. At the time, the company was around 25 people.

We started an aggressive outbound marketing campaign. We would mail two-by-three-foot custom cards to our prospects. These cards would have the names of our prospects printed on them and a link to a website built just for them. It was a massive effort. In one month alone, we sent almost 100 of these cards to a very targeted list of companies. We followed up by sending custom cakes and cupcakes and planned to touch base with these companies every month, whether they responded or not.

I remember sending emails to a large handful of people saying, "I'll be in New York next week if you are able to meet." I didn't actually have plans to be in New York when the emails were sent, but I would hop on a plane at a minute's notice when one responded with a yes. Long days and nights of prospecting were common.

At the time, we wondered when our efforts would pay off. We were doing everything we could just to get 15 minutes on the phone or an email response. The idea of closing a deal seemed far away.

Fast-forward two years and we are now a company of more than 60 and growing fast. We have a team of five in our different markets that are meeting daily with some of the coolest companies in the world. The other day, one of the founders and I were talking about our client list. We are working with the largest cosmetics company in the world, the largest hospitality company in the world, the largest online dating company in the world, and the list goes on. It seemed like this all happened overnight. One day I was prospecting with the hope of client meetings. The next I had so many contracts to sign that I couldn't keep up with the people wanting to do business.

Of course, this didn't happen overnight. It took two years of consistent, effective outreach every day to get to a point of momentum. It actually took five years when you consider that the three years before I joined the team had developed the success necessary to give us credibility when speaking with these large companies.

What you do once momentum hits can define your future. Ian McConnell is a beer brewer in Biddeford, Maine. He started the Banded Horn Brewing Company in 2013 after spending a year writing his business plan, finding investors, and building the brewery in a former mill space.

The company started with two employees, and that's where they were when they reached their goal of getting their beer distributed throughout Maine. This was their flywheel moment. Ian had been stepping consistently to get his business off the ground, and landing statewide distribution was the culmination of all that work.

"We could have stopped there," Ian said. "We would have been fine as a two-man team with distribution in bars and restaurants, but once the beer started to take off, I couldn't just sit there."

Ian could have taken a break and a raise once sales started to take off, but instead, he invested the earnings back into the company.

"I took the opportunity to expand our staff, invest in our brewery system, and start work on a tasting room."

By taking these steps, Ian changed his brewery's trajectory in a major way. Fast-forward two years, and Banded Horn now has bottle and can lines that are sold in stores in addition to the kegs that go to bars and restaurants. They also have a very active tasting room in the brewery that doubles as a community event space. And thanks to the additional manpower from expanding their staff, they've been able to grow distribution throughout New England. They've come a long way from that two-man shop when momentum first struck.

NEVER STOP STEPPING AND YOU WILL FIND YOURSELF IN A PERPETUAL CYCLE OF MOMENTUM.

Momentum makes it easier to push so keep pushing. Keep stepping. Never stop stepping and you will find yourself in a perpetual cycle of momentum. It's worth it!

The next few chapters will talk about things like teamwork, accountability, acceleration, and jump-starting your steps. These are all ways to keep momentum going so don't stop here . . . Keep going.

7
STEP TOGETHER: THE ROLE OF TEAMWORK

Teamwork is the ability to work together toward a common vision. The ability to direct individual accomplishments toward organizational objectives. It is the fuel that allows common people to attain uncommon results.

—Andrew Carnegie

Teamwork certainly isn't a new concept. Volumes have been written about it and just a quick Google search draws up endless bits of wisdom on the subject, with good reason: so much value comes from teamwork. Andrew Carnegie's definition especially ties into my motivation for writing this book. My goal is to help readers beat the odds and attain uncommon results no matter the starting place. The U.S. Navy SEALs have a team saying with a similar message: "Individuals play the game, but teams beat the odds." Alone it's possible, but with teamwork it's probable.

That said, you can't truly tap into the power of teamwork until you've taken major personal steps to put yourself in a position to win with a team. That's a big part of Step. Take Michael Jordan. He's often told stories about how he practiced for hours and hours every day when he was growing up. He dreamed of playing for North Carolina and winning championships, but he was actually cut from his high school basketball team. Even Michael Jordan needed to take the necessary steps to become the player he was. However, when he was ready to compete, he needed teammates like Scottie Pippen and Dennis Rodman to win.

We all need to work on ourselves—and work alone—before we try to leverage a team. I needed to write and work out my ideas for this book long before I shared it with the public, but what you are reading today is the result of teamwork. The team wasn't formed on day one, but as I started to take steps, it became obvious which other players I needed, and I began to look for them even as I continued to write. The product you are reading now is the result of a team of people who have jumped on board with the visions of Step. This book wouldn't be what it is without them.

For instance, my good friend Hannah Newlin was the very first person to read anything I had written and has been a confidant and encourager throughout the process.

There's also George Thomas. George was the guy who said, "Chris, finish the entire first draft on your own." He's also the guy who originally helped me outline the chapters so I had a map to follow whenever I became stuck and didn't know what else to write.

Then there were people like Marcus Ryan who helped me navigate finding the right editor and understanding the book market landscape. Then my wife, Amy, who made sacrifices both financially and in the form of time to make sure I was able to focus on my writing.

My editor, Maria Gagliano, helped by being the "take Chris's writings and make them make sense to people reading them" person. She is critical to the process of writing a book people will read. She carefully combs through what I write and helps to guide the writing in a way that makes it appealing and valuable to you, the audience.

This is what Maria does for a living. Were I to publish this book without a person like Maria on the team it might just get laughed off the shelf. It would probably look like amateur hour. There is a chance that years from now, after several books, I will probably get pretty good at this, which will make what she does easier, but it would be a major pitfall to go at this alone right now.

Micah Davis, Ethan Fisher, Mark Sterns, Ronnie Johnson, and many more people I'm leaving out have also helped in some shape or form to get me to the place where I could write the book you're reading today.

I'm very thankful to all of the people who have helped make my dream of encouraging people a reality. I couldn't do it without them. I realized very early on that I needed a team. I don't for a minute think I can do this on my own. I need a group of close friends to give honest feedback on the concept. I need people who will help me build the brand. I need people who are willing to introduce me to others and take a chance on a guy who has never published before. I need a team, and so do you.

When I started writing it was just me. I had to make that initial decision to start, but as I gained momentum, I quickly saw where I needed help and obtaining that help became a very important series of steps in the process.

I didn't find Maria until about a year and half into the process. I actually worked with several other people before getting to the place where Maria became a part of the team. There are still people who will be integral to the success of this book who aren't yet on the team and I can't wait to find them.

Please don't get me wrong—I'm not discounting your ability. I believe we all have the ability to accomplish truly amazing things if we follow the principles laid out in this book. The cool thing is how much more we can accomplish with a team.

When I was in high school, I read a biography about Henry Ford for a book report and I was fascinated by his life. In Napoleon Hill's *Think and Grow Rich*, he describes a time when a reporter had written an article saying that Ford was "an ignorant pacifist." Ford sued for libel and put himself on the stand to prove that he was indeed not.

The lawyers asked him all types of questions about history and current events. After getting a bit frustrated with the line of questioning, Ford pointed to the attorney and said:

If I should really want to answer the foolish question you have just asked, or any of the other questions you have been asking me, let me remind you that I have a row of electric push-buttons on my desk, and by pushing the right button, I can summon to my aid men who can answer any question I desire to ask concerning the business to which I am devoting most of my efforts. Now, will you kindly tell me, why I should clutter up my mind with general knowledge, for the purpose of being able to answer questions, when I have men around me who can supply any knowledge I require?

It's a funny story, but the point is he had a team. He didn't believe that he alone could know or accomplish everything relative to his pursuits. In fact, he didn't waste time learning things that he didn't believe mattered to his core pursuits. He had people around him to help accelerate his efforts and intellect as needed.

Who do you know who has taken similar steps before you and succeeded? Do you have someone on your team to do the tasks that otherwise will keep you from taking the most important steps?

Our team is our lifeline.

Build Your Team

If a team is such a critical component to success, how do we build one?

It starts with passion. Passion is contagious and it shows. Your vision should fire you up and it will come through in every conversation. Get good at sharing your vision and you'll be able to build a team. People want to be aligned with a big vision. We all want to go after things bigger than ourselves and we are just looking for the vehicle to take us there. Give people a clear vision and a clear way to see how they can contribute and you're on your way to creating a team.

GIVE PEOPLE A CLEAR VISION AND A CLEAR WAY TO SEE HOW THEY CAN CONTRIBUTE AND YOU'RE ON YOUR WAY TO CREATING A TEAM.

Passion for your vision is important, but passion for your team and their vision is of equal significance. Help people see how helping with your vision will ultimately take them to a place they want to be. We have to align our vision with those we want to join ours.

Jon Mitchell and his wife, Trina, would have never found their team and launched Zetêo Coffee if they hadn't constantly shared their vision with others. Jon and Trina had spent years researching, planning, and dreaming of opening a coffee shop, but they had trouble getting the logistics to work. The risks involved in opening their own space seemed too high for them to shoulder on their own. But they kept talking to friends and family about their dream, even when they had no idea how they'd be able to make it a reality.

They'd been sharing their vision for years when finally their world collided with another couple's, Craig and Erin Conner. The Conners were in the process of opening up an indoor play space called Share.the.Love Kid's Club. They had always wanted to include coffee service as part of their concept, but they didn't have the knowledge or capacity to build up that side of the business. But like the Mitchells, they kept talking to friends about their vision, including this little detail about coffee.

When a friend told the Conners that the Mitchells were eager to open a coffee shop, the Conners invited the Mitchells

> "

Help people see how helping with your vision will ultimately take them to a place they want to be.

CHRISCAPEHART.CO

Snap it, remember it, share it.

What does this statement mean to you?
Write it down.

_____

_____

_____

_____

CHRISCAPEHART.CO

Think about it, wrestle with it, do it.
#STEPBOOK

to join forces with them by opening Zetêo Coffee in their space.

It was the perfect scenario for all involved. Each company operates independently, but they're also a robust team with a shared customer base. The synergy between them has increased each company's abilities to market and attract customers that they would not have been able to reach on their own. They're also able to share the burdens of things like rent, which was always a hurdle when the Mitchells looked into launching Zetêo Coffee on their own.

If the Mitchells hadn't relentlessly shared their vision, the Conners would have never found them.

"There is a good chance that if we hadn't teamed up with the Conners and Share.the.Love Kid's Club, we would still be dreaming about Zetêo Coffee," Jon said. It was the addition of a team that made it possible for them to take the risk needed to open the business. A team wasn't just a "nice to have" for their dream, it was critical.

The best way to find a team is by starting with the people you already know. You'd be surprised how many people you interact with daily may also be looking for a vision to latch onto.

Look for people who are getting the results you want. We typically know who we aspire to be like in the field we are pursuing. Who is on their team? This is one of the most powerful questions I've asked during this process of writing the book. Who are on the teams of the authors I want to be like? Who are the mentors of the speakers I aspire to?

Once I've identified the dream team, which typically consists of people who have already done the thing I want to do, I go after them with thoughtful pursuit.

Thoughtful pursuit is critical to creating your dream team, especially if many others are already pursuing them. Instead of sending an email, send a cake. Instead of a cold call, how about a cold brew? A little social media stalking never hurt anyone. Find out what the person you want on your team likes and do a gesture that shows them you aren't just an ordinary person reaching out without a meaningful reason.

Ultimately, the path you choose in building your team will be unique to your pursuit. However, two critical components to building a team are passion and experience. When you find people who have both in the area you are pursuing, my suggestion would be to do everything in your power to make them a part of your team. People like this make an exponentially large contribution compared with those who lack this passion and experience.

The best part of winning with a team is getting to celebrate with them. What if I wrote this book all by myself and it was a huge hit? In fact, what if I won some big award and was flown in to receive it? What if I walked up on stage, took my trophy, and went back to an empty hotel room? That would suck!

I want to receive that reward with a table full of people who truly deserve the credit. I want to receive that reward on the behalf of a team. Then I want to call the people who couldn't make it to the ceremony and tell them, "We did it!" After that I want to spend all night with the group of people celebrating what I couldn't have done on my own.

SO GET OVER YOURSELF AND GET A TEAM. YOU'LL BE GLAD YOU DID.

Beyond the fact that it is difficult, if not impossible, to do anything meaningful without a team, it's simply not as rewarding. So get over yourself and get a team. You'll be glad you did.

8
ACCOUNTABILITY

I mentioned earlier that your team is your lifeline. This point's resonance grows with each step you take and as each member of your team helps you reach milestones that you didn't think were possible. Teams come in all stripes, and it doesn't matter what yours looks like as long as you have a reliable crew to help you reach your goals. Your team may be a squad of consultants and professionals or a single friend offering moral support. No matter its size, I want to highlight one of the most important gifts your team can give you: accountability.

The idea of accountability has been around for a long time and I have a feeling it's not going anywhere soon. There is a good reason for that—it works. Thomas Paine, in his writing *Rights of Man*, said it well: "A body of men holding themselves accountable to nobody ought not to be trusted by anybody."

These are the three key benefits I see from a great system of accountability:

1. Effectiveness: With great accountability our steps will be more effective because we will be pushed to do more than we believe we can accomplish.

2. Consistency: Continuing to step is a key to success and accountability provides the motivation we need to keep stepping.

3. Correctness: The right type of accountability can help us step in the right direction.

We won't ever step to our fullest potential if not challenged to increase our step. It doesn't matter how dedicated we may be to our goal. Just look at any Olympic athlete. We can't argue that anyone who has reached that level of success isn't extremely talented and dedicated to their sport. While their friends were sleeping in or playing, they spent their childhood practicing. But even with so much talent and drive, they couldn't do it on their own. They still had a coach who met them at the track (or pool, or skating rink) for every practice. That person pushed them to stick to their goals and to do more than they thought they were capable of achieving.

We all need someone to push us and to keep us honest, no matter how talented and dedicated we may be.

But let's throw out the word "accountability" for a second, because sometimes it has a negative connotation. The point is that we need perspective and honest assessment in the middle of anything—working out, writing a book, building a business, parenting a kid, getting through college, etc. We can never see our situation from every angle. We need the trusted perspective of someone on the outside to help assess whether what we are doing is enough or whether we're being true to the goal we're hoping to achieve.

WE ALL NEED SOMEONE TO PUSH US AND TO KEEP US HONEST, NO MATTER HOW TALENTED AND DEDICATED WE MAY BE.

We won't get stronger if we don't have anyone to tell us that we can do more when we feel like we're at the end of our rope. We won't produce great results if we are only relying on ourselves to produce them. Great accountability will push us to accomplish more than we could have believed. Take that to the bank of your future and you will be making a withdrawal when it counts.

Find Your Accountability Groove

Stepping's biggest enemy is stopping, especially if you don't have anybody asking you how you're doing. The more you make your commitment visible to others and seek accountability in maintaining your stride, the more likely you are to succeed.

We can't all have a dedicated coach, and most of us don't need one, but we can all use a friend, mentor, or just someone to talk to about our progress. The key to accountability is setting a consistent time to reflect and measure your efforts with someone other than yourself. You can have accountability through a phone call, Skype, face-to-face meeting, or even texts. The best accountability partners challenge our thinking and challenge our excuses. They provide encouragement while pushing us to do more.

What will work for you really depends on whom you are accountable to and where they are. One of my good friends has a monthly phone call with his accountability mentor. Mentors make great accountability partners because they typically have more experience than we do and they've accomplished something that we desire. They know the road ahead and can help us gauge whether our efforts align with our desired outcome.

Accountability can also come in groups. Some say that a common cause of divorce is financial disagreement. I would agree. Finances play a role in almost everything we do or can't do! It could be argued that you have financial accountability with your spouse—or you should. However, I think most couples would agree that we could use a neutral third party to keep us accountable. Have you ever thought of having a group of closely trusted "couple" friends to do a monthly financial report? We do this at work and in any company setting. We have to keep ourselves accountable to the goals we set. If we don't hit our goals or budgets, we have to explain ourselves. And sometimes we get fired. Why not have "trusted friends" keep a couple accountable to the goals they have set?

I'm not suggesting you share every piece of your financial information with your friends. I'm only suggesting that we should look for ways to have accountability as individuals, as couples, as businesses, etc. This type of accountability can help mitigate arguments and provide a neutral voice to help an entity (more than one person) stay on track with their steps.

My friend Maria has accountability by combining a calendar with weekly phone calls. She lives in New Jersey and runs a nonprofit called Slice with her co-director, Celia Johnson, who lives in Maine. The pair spends all year planning the Slice Literary Writers' Conference. Each director has mapped out her steps in a shared calendar, which they review by phone every week. This helps them pace their progress leading up to the big event, and it keeps them accountable to one another.

"If it's the day before our phone call and I haven't stepped in a few days, I make sure I catch up so that I'm ready for our call," Maria said. "If I don't step, it may hold Celia back if she's counting on me to complete part of a shared project. And privately, I just don't want my friend and business partner to think I'm a slacker! I also really do want to accomplish great things through this conference, and the accountability reminds me of the goals I've set for myself."

The calendar also serves as a neutral third party. Maria and Celia can go down the list of action items and discuss their progress without having to put each other on the spot.

Sometimes accountability doesn't come in the form of a good friend, but as a tough boss or manager. Jennifer is a sales executive for a software company. She has been working at the company for three years and has hit all of her goals. Her book of business is solid and she is pretty much able to run her quotas without too much extra effort. Jennifer worked her butt off the first year and is enjoying the fruits of her labor.

But Jennifer's boss recently left the company and she is a bit concerned about her new manager, John. The second week on the job John tells Jennifer that her quota for the next year is going to be increased by 15%. Jennifer is, as they say in the South, "cussin' mad."

After a few choice words in her mind, Jennifer starts to think back to how she built the business two years earlier. She starts making phone calls and prospecting. She gets back to work. By the end of the year, Jennifer not only hit the 15% mark but she passed it and grew her business by 30%. She took home an additional $30,000 in commission, which gave her the extra money she needed to redo her kitchen. Not only that, since John pushed her team to grow sales by 15% and the company was successful, her stock options are now worth that much more.

In her yearly review with John, she tells him how mad she was when he came with this bump and quota, but now she could not be happier. John just smiles and says, "I knew you had it in you. I knew it would be tough, but that you would love the results."

Jennifer's story is so close to many of ours. It is the friend, boss, or spouse that challenges us to be better. We struggle with the challenge, but rise to the occasion, and the results on the other end are breathtaking. Great rewards usually do not come without some type of sacrifice, but typically the sacrifice seems like nothing when you're looking back. After all it was just one step at a time.

I'm a little over a year and a half into writing this book and it looks like it will end up taking two years to have the final product on the market. I originally had a plan to make that happen in a year. One of the main reasons it has taken longer is because I didn't seek out the level of accountability that I should have. I lost momentum with my steps and lost time when it came to getting the book where it needed to be for public consumption. I have no one to blame but myself. We can all fall prey to not pushing for accountability as hard as we push for our goals.

Asking Someone to Be Your Accountability Partner

When you ask someone to help keep you on track, you are asking them for a commitment of time and effort. You're inviting them to proactively challenge and encourage you to move beyond your self-imposed limitations.

I recommend asking someone who you trust and who you know cares about the outcome of your life. It might be a close friend or a loved one, but it could also be a coworker or a boss. Ideally that person will have a track record of sticking to commitments. You wouldn't want to ask someone to help keep you accountable if they already have trouble staying focused in their own life.

Since you're asking this person for quite the commitment, I suggest finding a mutually beneficial reason for why they would want to help you keep on track. In other words, they could probably use someone committed to helping them in the same way. My most successful allies have been people who shared the need and desire for accountability in some area of their own life.

The conversation is easy when this is the case and goes something like this:

"Mike, we are both pursuing a promotion in our respective departments. I think we could help each other by meeting twice a month to encourage and challenge one another to make sure we are doing everything possible to deserve the promotion."

Or . . .

"Angie, I know you've been wanting to start blogging consistently, and I'm wanting to work out on a more consistent basis, so what if we texted each other twice a week to see how each person is doing?"

Or one of my favorites . . .

"Dave, we both have been talking about being proactive to plan a very special date with our wives each month. Let's email each other the details of our date on a monthly basis and if one of us doesn't do it, we have to pay for the other's date the next month."

Here are the three things I recommend setting in place with your accountability partner:

Consistent touch point. Whether it's through coffee, text, email, phone call, or repeating calendar invite, find a consistent time or way to connect. If this isn't agreed upon and set in place from the very beginning, you're setting yourself up for failure. During your time to connect, be honest about what you've done and what you haven't.

Perspective review: the why. When you didn't do what you had committed to doing, talk about what you are sacrificing—or better yet allow your partner to remind you about what you are sacrificing. If your step was saving money in order to pay for your children's college and you fell off track, talk about what it's going to feel like to let your child know that you won't be able to help them with tuition. If you have stepped faithfully, talk about what it's going to feel like to take your child to college registration and let them know that you're helping to cover the bill.

Optional: consequences. I'm a big fan of consequences to not stepping. These can be fun and motivating at the same time. Take the example above about Dave and paying for your date if he didn't take his wife out the previous month.

When I was younger and single, I had two friends who decided to make a commitment that each time they didn't do the thing they had committed to doing they would tear up a $100 bill and throw it in the garbage. These guys weren't rich by any means so this hurt, but you better believe it made them think twice about not continuing to step.

I think consequences add an enormous level of fun and commitment to step. If you're not willing to put some consequences in place, you may not be ready to fully commit to your dream.

Find accountability. It can be the difference between taking the next step or stopping. It can be the difference between being the person you have dreamed about or living with regret. Let your team challenge you. I give you permission to be mad at the challenge so long as you're not mad at the person. They are doing what's best for you.

9
THE RIGHT STEP

I hope you've already started stepping by now. If you're anything like me, you may have started working toward your first steps the moment you sat down with this book. I'm the type of person who loves to leap first and ask questions later. I've always believed that you just need to start taking action. However, this attitude has its pros and cons and it may not be for everyone.

During my time at ROOV.com, I was partners with two of my best friends, Ethan Fisher and Micah Davis. We were three very unique people with different attitudes and perspectives when it came to action. One day Micah described the three of us.

He said, "Chris likes to jump and ask questions later; I'll ask a few questions before I jump; and Ethan is going to do the most due diligence before he moves."

Micah's assessment was spot-on and honestly very beneficial. Though each one of us could make a great point for why our methods of action were better than the others', we realized there was great value in each. We also realized that it's best to approach a project with a blend of both caution and action, so you're never sitting idle or moving blindly in the wrong direction.

Throughout this book, I've encouraged you to start stepping. We've talked about breaking down your goals into steps and how that process works, but my biggest hope is that you simply get going. There's just one caveat to my advice, and it's to make sure you're going in the right direction.

Let's say you want to become a coffee roaster and eventually open up your own coffee shop. You don't know anything about the industry, but you're eager to get started and learn as you go. This is a great attitude (it's usually how I approach things!), but before you spend money on a roaster, supplies, and all of the necessary elements to start this venture, please make sure you do your due diligence.

>> **66**

Understanding what not to do can be just as important as knowing what to do.

CHRISCAPEHART.CO

Snap it, remember it, share it.

#STEPBOOK

What does this statement mean to you?
Write it down.

_____

_____

_____

_____

CHRISCAPEHART.CO

Think about it, wrestle with it, do it.
#STEPBOOK

First, find someone in the industry more knowledgeable than you and listen. Ask for advice, ask about the craft, and research the craft. Do as much online research as you can, but also get out there and talk to people who have accomplished what you're setting out to do. These are steps just like any others we've been talking about, but they're learning steps. They're the "due diligence" phase of your step process. When an investor is considering backing a new company, one of the first things they will do is due diligence.

Jon Mitchell enrolled in an intensive coffee and barista course in Portland, Oregon, during his due diligence phase of launching Zetêo Coffee. "I'd never worked in a coffee shop or really had much of any experience even fixing coffee in a coffee maker for that matter," he said. He knew that in order to take the right steps, he needed quality training.

This is a critical phase because it will allow you to find out what the right steps are before you waste time doing the wrong ones. Remember, we have a finite amount of time, resources, and energy. Steps need to give us the biggest bang for our buck and this is one of the best ways to ensure that. Learn from the mistakes of others. Most of the time people are more than happy to share their mistakes with those who ask for their advice. Understanding what not to do can be just as important as knowing what to do. Let's go back to our coffee roaster example. What if you jumped right in and started spending all of your money buying different coffee machines and mini roasters. You produced the product, but it just wasn't what you had in mind. Finally, in despair, you asked for help from someone who knew what they were doing.

In five minutes, they pointed out that the roaster you had was not the best for the job and recommended something else. But since you've already spent your money on the current roaster you're going to need to save for six more months in order to buy the right equipment, or go through the hassle of selling the one you have. If you had asked someone first, you could have saved yourself time and money and been closer to your goals.

The best way to understand what steps you need to take is by talking to others who have already reached the place you are trying to go. They are usually able to provide invaluable insight about your pursuit and can save you months or even years of stumbling and learning things the hard way.

If you don't already know someone who has done what you are trying to do, get online. Perhaps you'll find a Facebook group for whatever you're trying to do, which might include highly experienced people. LinkedIn will also be a great resource for finding potential mentors. Just make sure to research the people from whom you are learning, wherever you find them.

Be excited to ask for help. It just might be the best step you've ever taken. I've found in multiple scenarios that when I genuinely ask for help people are more than happy to oblige. You may get the occasional person who doesn't want to talk to you, but that's rare. Remember to place all of your ideas on the floor and listen. I have to admit that sometimes I've asked for advice, but secretly thought I knew the answer to the question. I was doing it as more of a formality. This is stupid. If you are going to take the time to ask for advice, then take the time to listen. Every piece of advice you get may not be for you, but you can decide that later.

BE EXCITED TO ASK FOR HELP. IT JUST MIGHT BE THE BEST STEP YOU'VE EVER TAKEN.

Placing yourself around people who are where you want to be can also open up opportunities. There's nothing wrong with that. Just make sure your motives are right. People can sniff someone seeking a handout and that's not what I'm talking about.

Keep Stepping in the Right Direction

I believe in starting to step immediately instead of waiting. I also believe in taking wise steps, so make sure you consult the experts early in your journey to ensure your steps are taking you where you want to go. In some cases, your first step is research or advice gathering. In some situations, your first step is to get started with an action and also start pursuing wise counsel. In writing this book, I didn't wait to talk with an editor before I started to write. I just jumped into writing because I had a concept to write about. However, I immediately started researching and looking for people who could help guide me to create a better book. I read articles from authors. I met with people to validate the concept and I met with people who write books for a living. I was doing all of this at the same time.

The beauty of the Step process is that it's simple to figure out what step to take. You don't need someone to tell you every single step; you just need someone to help you make sure you're stepping in the right direction. Don't worry if you've been stepping for a while and are starting to wonder whether you're on the right path. It's never too late to ask for a little guidance. It's also OK if you find out you have been taking the wrong steps. You found out and now you can change course. Taking the wrong steps for the right reasons is always better than not taking steps at all. Courses can be corrected, but there is not a silver bullet for inaction.

You'll likely find that the people you ask for advice will be impressed to see that you have done more than just think about an idea. Let's go back to the concept of investing. People are more likely to invest money in something that is already off the ground rather than a brand-new idea. In the same way, people are more willing to invest time into a person who is taking steps than a person who is just pondering an idea.

YOU DON'T NEED SOMEONE TO TELL YOU EVERY SINGLE STEP; YOU JUST NEED SOMEONE TO HELP YOU MAKE SURE YOU'RE STEPPING IN THE RIGHT DIRECTION.

Once you find trusted advisors, know that the advice will continue if you act on their suggestions. If you continue to ask for advice with no action, people will be less willing to spend time helping you. Like most companies, we have an advisory board at Oven Bits. The people on our advisory board also sit on numerous other boards. The one thing they have said multiple times is how happy they are to give their time to a group of people that actually do what they suggest.

Sometimes it's hard to hear what your advisors have to say. One of the best pieces of advice I received was to write the book myself. It was also one of the more discouraging pieces of advice I heard. At the time I had written amounts to about 35% of the book (the first few chapters). I'd never written this much before and I was pretty proud of myself for getting this far.

I met with my friend George Thomas, who writes for a living. I was hoping he would tell me that because of the base I'd written it would be pretty easy for a ghostwriter to finish it out. I was thinking this book thing really isn't all that hard. I'd written for a few months and complete the for me I was wrong.

George urged me to finish the book myself. He said I should create the content and then get someone's help editing to make it better. That's not what I wanted to hear. I wanted to hear that I was almost done. He continued, saying the book would be better and more genuine to the message I wanted to get across if I went this direction.

I'm so glad I listened to him. If I hadn't, I would have found someone to finish the book for me and I know it would have been disappointing. Just the feeling of accomplishment alone was worth pushing through, and in the end, I believe the finished book truly reflects everything I wanted it to.

This is a great example of taking the right steps. I could have hired a ghostwriter as my next step, but instead, I finished the entire first draft on my own. I believe that writing the book myself will be a big factor in its success. It also makes a big difference to me when putting my name and finances behind it. The point I want to make is that you can start without knowing much and in parallel protect yourself by making sure you're taking the right step.

Also know that you can only get so far by asking people for free advice. As I mentioned, most people will gladly share their experiences with you, but sometimes you'll find that you need more than a little wisdom—you need hands-on help. Consultants can be a good option in these scenarios. When I hired an editor to help finalize this book, she ultimately served as a consultant. Most companies have hired a consultant at one time or another to help guide them. A consultant is someone with specific experience doing the thing you are trying to accomplish. At Oven Bits, we're currently working with a consultant who we hired to help us through the PCI certification process. PCI certification is important for any type of technology that deals with credit cards. It's not an easy process and even for a company it can be overwhelming. We have to walk through 200-page reports that detail how to handle security. Sure, we could have someone in our company figure out how to put together all of the necessary information the auditors need, but how long would it take? And what if there are some critical things that we overlook because we didn't even know to look for them? A consultant who has helped to certify 100 companies can guide us through everything we need to do with accuracy. The money we spend will be more than saved in the headache and time it would take to figure this out on our own.

LinkedIn is a great resource for finding consultants in your field. Keep in mind that you don't have to go through a mega consulting firm, which can be daunting and expensive. Many people work as independent consultants after being in their field for several years. If you've already found a highly experienced person to give you advice, they may be willing to work with you on a closer level as a consultant. Just ask them. If they can't do it, they'll likely be able to refer you to one of their colleagues. Most consultants find their work through word of mouth, so ask around and don't hold back just because someone doesn't promote themselves as a "consultant." That said, be willing to move on quickly if someone says they won't do it. Not everyone with extensive experience is cut out to be a consultant. It requires time, patience, and a knack for teaching, so if someone is turning you down they likely can't offer each of these critical qualities. Just keep working the referral engine until you find the right fit.

Let me be clear: This chapter does not give you permission to spend endless months researching and never taking any real action. It gives you permission to add the element of advice to your step process. Due diligence doesn't last forever. If it did, a company would never get bought and you would never accomplish your dreams.

10
ACCELERATE YOUR STEP

There may come a time when you need and/or want to accelerate your step. Perhaps you're at place where you can see the finish line and realize that with a bit of a push you could get there in a quarter of the time it would take at your current pace. Or you might just feel the need for a shot of adrenaline to reinvigorate and motivate you to keep going. We all want to move fast toward our goals and this chapter will help you amp up the pace.

There are four major ways to accelerate your step and each one plays a role at different points on your journey. You'll likely tap into all of them at least once through the course of your mile.

The four ways to accelerate your step are time, team, learning, and kick-start.

Time

You can accelerate your step by shrinking the amount of time you take to get to the finish line. This won't reduce the amount of work that needs to be done (if you want to run a mile you'll always have to cover the same distance), but it will help you reach your goal sooner. The difference is in how many steps you take at a time and how often or how fast you take those steps.

I've mentioned that in writing this book, I started by writing one hour twice a week. That's all I could do and it was perfectly fine. However, there came a point several months in that my passion for finishing started to increase and I wanted to find ways to write more. I wanted desperately to get this content into the hands of people I believed it could help. I started meeting with several people who are better at writing than I am. I asked them how I could accelerate the process. I looked at ghostwriting opportunities, editors, and other forms of freelance writers. The best advice I received was to get more content written before I went into editing. My wife and I agreed that it was time for me to put more effort into finishing this book, so I spent half a day writing. Over the weekend, my wife took care of our daughter. My goal was to spend four hours writing. Those four hours equaled two full weeks of my regular steps. In one day, I accelerated my step by at least two weeks.

My drive to work is about one hour each way. I spent a week using a voice-to-text program to write during some of that time as well. I was motivated and could see the finish line. When I started this process I felt like I was never going to get to the end, but I believed in the power of Step, so I started. After several months of consistent steps, although there were a few bumps along the way, I had written the basis for five or six chapters and was well on my way to having a solid base for the book.

We all have different capacities and different time availability. There is not a right or wrong level of Step. Like I said, we all have to cover the same distance to go a mile. Someone may run that mile in four minutes while it might take someone else three hours. Your general pace doesn't matter, but you can increase the speed and frequency of your steps when you want to kick things up a notch.

Our lives are busy. I can guarantee that if I ask 10 people how things are going, at least nine of them will say, "Busy, it's just been really busy lately." I find myself saying this all the time. It's been 10 years now and my answer hasn't changed. Finding time to accelerate your step can seem impossible, but here are a couple of ideas that might help:

TV time. I value my TV time. It's how I unwind and relax after a hard day. A big glass of my favorite beverage, some DVRed shows, and I'm off to relaxation. There are quite a few nights that I will find myself spending two hours watching TV and not accomplishing anything productive. I tell myself that I'm too tired to do anything else, but the reality is I just don't want to. I could, though. I took the weekend to write for four extra hours, but what if I gave up my TV time two nights a week? I'd accelerate my step that much faster. Is there TV time you could sacrifice for the sake of your beautiful dream?

Social media. Most of us spend at least a few minutes each day scrolling through our social media feeds. It's easy to get lost clicking through pictures, and suddenly you're watching cat videos on your ex-girlfriend's Facebook timeline. Those little breaks add up at an alarming rate. If you're trying to find time to step more frequently, try going cold turkey on social media. You'll be amazed at how free you feel, and how you suddenly have a little more time to squeeze in an extra 20 minutes to work on your dream.

We need to reclaim wasted time in our day. While I was on the road at a conference, my team went out to dinner and I stayed behind to write. I found time because I questioned what really mattered and prioritized accordingly. There was no good or bad to come from missing this dinner, so I took the opportunity away from home to accelerate my steps.

Your time is finite, but if you're eager to keep your step moving, you'll be able to find extra pockets of time to reach your goal. If you work out for 30 minutes three days a week, try for 45 minutes or an hour. If you work on your novel two days a week, aim for three, or increase your time for each session. Perhaps this means waking up earlier or taking less time for lunch, but it will be worth it.

WE NEED TO RECLAIM WASTED TIME IN OUR DAY.

My grandfather is incredible when it comes to finding margin in his day. He does this by being efficient with his time. Don't expect to sit down and have a nice long lunch with Stan. There aren't too many lunches I can remember that lasted longer than 15 minutes. He also doesn't drink coffee explicitly because he doesn't want to waste time on daily coffee breaks. Now, I'm a fan of coffee and enjoying lunch, but Stan had a vision and between these two seemingly simple hacks he would save an hour and 15 minutes each day. If you do this for a week, you have almost a whole extra day. Whether or not his examples work for you, the point is that there are ways to find extra time to increase our step if we look close.

Team

We've talked about the importance of having a team to help you achieve your goals. In fact, a team is one of the best ways to accelerate your step beyond your own ability or time. You can lean on others to help accelerate your step in two core ways:

Have someone help cover your other responsibilities so you can spend more time stepping. This can work on many levels. It can be short-term support, like when my wife cared for our daughter while I wrote over the weekend. If you're looking for a consistent block of free time, try to think about how you spend your week, and what you can outsource. Do you spend two hours every Saturday mowing the lawn? If you have the budget to hire someone else to do it, you can accelerate your step by dedicating that extra two hours to stepping. This is a version of using time to accelerate your step, as I described above, only you're tapping into a team for longer-term help.

Bring in a team to help work on your step. In this case, your team is actually working on your step with you to help accelerate the process. Perhaps you've been making steady progress toward your goal to lose 50 pounds by losing five pounds a month, but you want to do more. You can work with a personal trainer to optimize your workout, or a nutritionist to make sure your eating habits are in line with your goal.

If you're working on a big project and wearing many hats, think about what you may be able to delegate to others so that you can put more time and energy into the work that matters most to your goal. In my case, I brought in a team to help market my book so I could spend more time actually writing it, and writing it quickly.

What are you trying to do on your own that is taking up too much of your time? Can you bring in someone else to do it better, and faster, so that you can do the same for your core tasks?

Or if you're truly the only one who can do the work, how can someone else lend support so you can put more time and effort into stepping?

Think of how a team can help you so you can continue to accelerate your step.

Learning

As we step, we should learn more about the steps we are taking. As we learn more about the steps we are taking, we can learn how to better take those steps.

When I first began writing this book, I simply started writing. I had a general plan in my mind for the direction I was going to take the book and I just started going. I had no clue what the next chapter would be until I got there. This worked well enough, but eventually I was spending more time trying to figure out where I'd go next than I was actually writing. Finally, I sat down and wrote an outline for the book. The outline served as a map so that I knew exactly what I was sitting down to write each time. It was a lesson I had learned through the course of this mile that allowed me to focus on writing during my weekly steps instead of thinking about what I should write. There's no telling how much that advanced my step.

In the online world, we call this optimization. We launch a website or an app and bake in all types of analytics to let us know how people are using the tools we've put in their hands. We constantly look at the results of those analytics and make decisions about changes to the design, flows, etc., to better serve the ultimate goal, whatever it may be.

The key here is to optimize—and accelerate—our step by learning as we go. Reading articles or tips about how to most effectively do the thing you are doing is a great way to learn how to optimize your step for maximum efficiency.

I also suggest regularly evaluating your step's output and asking whether the step is moving you as fast as you believe it should.

What once took me an hour may now only take me 30 minutes, and I've just doubled my time to step because I learned from the previous steps taken. It's much quicker to use a calculator for large equations than pencil and paper. What is the calculator for your step?

Kick-Start

When I ran cross-country in high school, I was extremely disciplined about pacing myself. I didn't want to start too fast and use all of my energy. Evidently, I didn't know it all and one day my coach pulled me aside. He taught me a very valuable lesson. He told me that I should start the race as fast as I could run. He said, "Get ahead of everyone in the first 200 meters and then slow down into your race pace."

He explained that it takes a lot of energy to navigate the race in the first few hundred meters because so many other runners are on the path with you. He said I should start my race at a very fast pace so I can get in front of the crowd. Once I had a clear path, I could slow down into my race pace, and at that point I wouldn't have to elbow through so many people. The other reason was that it takes less energy to slow down than speed up. Implementing this what I thought to be counterintuitive strategy in my racing made a huge difference.

My coach was advising me to kick-start my race. This is a concept we can apply to just about anything, and it's especially useful when you want to accelerate your step from a standstill to a healthy pace of accomplishment.

A kick-start is the act of stepping at a pace that is not sustainable in order to move you past the place of starting or beyond a place of being stuck. It's a short-term jolt to help you move things quickly, whether you need a fast start or you want to breathe new life into a lull. I find myself doing some form of a kick-start every few months.

You can kick-start your project in two core ways: with time and effort, or with funding.

I kick-started this book using time and effort. At first I didn't take time off work to start writing the book; I started slow and steady. My kick-start came a bit later when I took a week off to dedicate 50 hours to finalizing a draft to send to my editor. At my typical pace (two hours per week), it would have taken almost six months to accomplish what I did in that one week. I needed a kick-start if I wanted to finish my book in the timeline I was hoping for.

Focus is a critical benefit of the kick-start. Being able to focus on the book for an entire week created momentum that I wish I'd had all the time. Now this dedicated time didn't come without a cost. The week I took off could have been used for lounging at the pool or going on a vacation with my family. Instead, I woke up early and went to bed late. I basically worked an entire week during my vacation, but it was worth it.

A financial kick-start can also be a great help, especially when you're just starting. When Chase and Cambryn decided to get out of debt, they gave themselves a major kick-start by selling Chase's Land Cruiser. This one transaction allowed them to pay off the loan on Cambryn's car and buy another car for Chase in cash. It also lowered their bills since they no longer had to make a monthly payment on Cambryn's car or spend so much to fill the gas-guzzling Land Cruiser.

Chase and Cambryn were stepping at a non-sustainable pace when they sold the Land Cruiser because it was a single opportunity to knock out a major portion of their debt. Unless they had other big possessions to sell, their next steps would be smaller and at a steadier pace, but their kick-start helped them make huge progress in one big swoop.

The crowd-funding website Kickstarter, and many others like it, do this very thing. They help people crowd-source a financial kick-start to get their project off the ground. The Mitchells and the Conners created an Indiegogo campaign to fund the launch of Zetêo Coffee and Share.the.Love Kid's Club, and millions of others are tapping into crowd-funding every year.

I encourage you to look for opportunities to use these methods to accelerate your step. It's a great way to take a massive leap forward in a short amount of time, not to mention the residual effects of excitement and enthusiasm that tend to follow a period of increased productivity. These accelerations do not have to last forever. They're meant to be short bursts to get you from one milestone to the next, or to help you kick off a new part of your mile.

You are the master of your own step. You get to dictate when and how fast you accelerate. I'll leave you with one question:

How can you accelerate your step today?

11
BALANCE

There is a good chance you've heard someone make the statement, "When you get old, you won't wish you'd spent more time at work." This book is meant to help you get to where you want to be. I think it's important that we examine how to balance the desire to achieve with achieving the things that truly matter.

The goals I talk about in this book are all over the map because we each want to achieve different things in all aspects of life. But if I were to ask each of my readers to give me their top five goals that they intend to step toward, I would be willing to bet that "make more money" would show up on just about everyone's list.

It may take the form of getting a promotion, starting a business, or some other variation.

This is a noble goal. Most of us want to provide more for our families. I just want to give our families a fair shake when it comes to how we prioritize and plan the steps. It's likely that the steps you need to take to accomplish your goal will cause you to spend less time with your family. This isn't only true for financial goals. It can apply to working out, volunteering, and many other goals that could be brought to life through reading this book.

This book's main point is that you can work toward a goal in small bursts. I ask that when creating your steps, you don't forget the plan to care for and love your family with the same ferocity that you go after any other mile or goal. I don't believe that a family should suffer at the hands of a goal. For those of you who don't yet have a family or plan to have one in the future, please stay with me. This still applies.

You will never get the chance to hold your infant daughter once she grows up. There will only be so many baseball and soccer games. We should all be taking steps to put the first thing in our lives first. For most of us, family is something that takes one of the top spots.

The flip side of this is that there may be some level of sacrifice to produce the ultimate goal. For instance, if you want to pay off your debt, it may require taking an extra job on the weekends. Starting your own business could require some long hours and that's OK. There are times when we have to make sacrifices, but it shouldn't be all the time.

I ASK THAT WHEN CREATING YOUR STEPS, YOU DON'T FORGET THE PLAN TO CARE FOR AND LOVE YOUR FAMILY WITH THE SAME FEROCITY THAT YOU GO AFTER ANY OTHER MILE OR GOAL.

We need to live our lives while we can. I personally have this challenge because when I get focused on accomplishing a goal, I have the tendency to tune everything else out and just run. I will come home at night after spending 10 or 12 hours away from the house and place a high importance on checking my email or doing some extra work. There may be a few times here and there that warrant this type of commitment, but I shouldn't live this way forever. Life is too short and fleeting to give it up for a few extra bucks or the approval of a boss.

I have the feeling you probably won't think this is a stupid idea. Most of us don't want to work more and spend more time away from home. But it can be hard to manage pursuing your goals and still have time to prioritize the rest of life. Before I give some examples of how you might achieve this, let me say that your accountability team can play a big role. Sometimes it takes outside perspective to help jump-start our minds in a certain direction. I can't tell you how many times I've struggled to find the answer to something I'm working on, and as soon as I've shared it with someone I trust, they've suggested a clear solution. It happens quite a bit with my wife! Please don't tell her I admitted that. I'm still trying to keep up an image.

Let's say you need to work out more, but you don't want to spend any extra time away from your family. What can you do?

You could work out during your lunch hour. More and more people are doing this. Remember we can take steps. Your workout could be a walk. It doesn't have to be at a gym. Another great idea is doing one of the many popular home workouts. One step I started taking toward working out more was the "seven-minute workout challenge." When my daughter was one year old, she loved to watch me work out in the living room. She laughed the whole time and in her own way tried to help. Sometimes during my push-ups, she would come over and push me down every time I'd come up. Though she was just a little girl, that extra pressure sure made those push-ups tougher!

What about the idea of starting your own business or trying to do extra work to get ahead at your current company?

The easiest answer is to take your steps when your family is asleep. This may mean doing things super early or super late. It might also mean organizing your day in a way that allows you to dedicate early mornings or late nights to your project. In order to get out of the house early enough to work on this book, I had to have all of my clothes ironed and laid out the night before. I also prepared breakfast the night before. I would wake up, work out, take a shower, grab breakfast, and leave the house in 45 minutes or less in order to get to the coffee shop where I wrote by 7 a.m. This took some planning and adjusting of my normal routine, but if you are passionate enough about it, you can figure out how to make it work.

Another thing I do is figure out how to be more efficient and better organized to accomplish things that truly matter. There are great books out there about productivity and efficiency. I think everyone should read *The 4-Hour Workweek* by Timothy Ferriss. Whether or not you agree with the premise of everything he says, some of the ideas and principles for efficiency are great. At the heart of his book, he talks about leverage and how outsourcing work can be a great way to get more done in the same amount of time or less. Just recently, I was talking with a good friend of mine about how I was going to market this book. I laid out my plan and he looked at me with one of those "Are you crazy?" looks. He said, "Chris, how are you going to find the time to do all of this plan you laid out? You need to hire someone."

When it comes to marketing I feel pretty good about my abilities. This is what I do for a living. However, I had created a plan that needed an additional 15 hours a week of my time to execute. The tasks were not necessarily complex. It included things like scheduling social media and cueing up email updates. I could hire someone to do this. I had been so stuck in the mindset of not wanting to spend any extra money on things I could do that I forgot doing those things might actually cost me the success I desired. Actually, what had been happening is that the marketing activities were taking a backseat to writing— they weren't getting done, so the book had the risk of not getting seen. This would defeat the entire purpose of writing it. Thanks to my friend's perspective and great advice from guys like Tim Ferriss, I was able to bring some balance back into my life by outsourcing tasks. When you look into it, you'll find that getting virtual assistants or perhaps even students to help with these types of tasks can be quite cost-effective. Eat a few more meals at home and you can afford to outsource a few hours of work each week that will give you the time needed to focus on what matters.

Finding an extra two hours in a day may be difficult, but 15 minutes can be found with a bit of reengineering and focus. I find most of the things we do for work typically don't get us to our ultimate goal. Why do we do them?

I already mentioned that my grandfather doesn't drink coffee in order to save time. He once explained the full reason behind this decision. He told me that he didn't understand how people who drank coffee could be successful. I remember laughing because I drink coffee and my grandmother, his wife, drinks coffee. He unpacked it a little more for me. He told me a story about some of his old colleagues with whom he used to do sales calls. They couldn't do anything before they had their coffee, but it wasn't good enough to just get a cup of coffee. They needed sugar and milk and who knows what else. He said it would take these guys 30 minutes at least twice a day to get their coffee fix. "In that wasted hour," he said, "I could be making sales and progress toward my goals." The point wasn't the coffee—it was the procrastination. My grandfather spent time away from his family for work and he was going to use every minute to get ahead. He thought it was pointless to waste time. Now I'm sure we coffee drinkers aren't all doomed, but it's worth evaluating where we spend our time to see if we are being effective or just getting by being comfortable.

Stan made sure to use his time efficiently at work, but he knew that wasn't enough to find balance. He spent a lot of evenings and weekends taking steps to put his family in the financial position he desired. This was time he took from his family; however, he found balance by drawing a line when it came to supporting his kids' extracurricular activities. He had three girls and one boy. They all rodeoed at one time or another. Three of them played basketball and my mom was a cheerleader. He didn't miss an opportunity to show his kids the support they needed by being present.

Stan set a boundary that he wouldn't let his work or desire for a better financial life cross. In his mind, being present at his kids' games was just as important as being out pursuing the next deal. There is a balance and we have to find it.

I strongly believe where there is a desire there is a way to find time to take steps and keep balance. I like to apply the 80/20 rule as much as possible and I think it's worth mentioning here. If your life is in balance 80% of the time, you're probably doing a good job. There will always be those 20% moments where you have to pull an all-nighter or spend an extended amount of time and effort to jump-start a project, business, or goal, as we talked about in the previous chapter.

I STRONGLY BELIEVE WHERE THERE IS A DESIRE THERE IS A WAY TO FIND TIME TO TAKE STEPS AND KEEP BALANCE.

Even if your schedule is jam-packed, you can find time for your family, and for your step. Again, I talked earlier about stealing time from social media browsing. This alone can be a powerful change. Social media and general web surfing drain a lot of time from our day. You may be shocked to find how much time you suddenly have if you get off the web, or at least limit your usage throughout the day. You don't have to go cold turkey, but try taking small measures, like deleting social media apps from your phone or just simply turning off notifications. Now, rather than sinking your nose into your phone and letting

20 minutes melt away, you can work out or eat dinner with your family or do whatever else you swear you don't have enough time to do.

Your time is finite, and it is precious. Make sure you're spending it in ways that help you create the life you want. If you're still at a loss about how to find time to fuel your dream, a great book to check out is *What the Most Successful People Do Before Breakfast* by Laura Vanderkam. It offers a great glimpse into how others find the time to achieve their goals, and everyone in the book lives a rich, balanced life. Vanderkam makes the case that mornings are the best time to pursue major life ambitions, before the rest of our day's responsibilities kick in. She explains that "the best morning rituals . . . are activities that require internal motivation. The payoff isn't as immediate as the easy pleasure of watching television or answering an email that doesn't require an immediate response, but there are still payoffs. The best morning rituals are activities that, when practiced regularly, result in long-term benefits." Her research shows that the most successful people use their mornings to nurture their careers, nurture their relationships, and nurture themselves.

Now I've talked quite a bit about family in this chapter and some of my single readers may be thinking this doesn't apply to them. Quite the contrary. Replace every time I wrote the word "family" with the word "friend," or "relationships," or "people."

Accomplishing things alone is not fun. Sacrificing your life to accomplish something and not being able to enjoy it with others is not worth it. I've seen people gain enormous success at the expense of their family and friends. You don't have to do this to get what you desire. You can find balance. You just have to make finding it a priority.

When you lay out your plan to step, make relationships a high priority and take steps toward making them great. It will be worth it. If you are reading this book and realizing that you have failed in this area, that's OK. It's never too late to start taking steps toward creating lasting relationships with the ones we love the most.

SACRIFICING YOUR LIFE TO ACCOMPLISH SOMETHING AND NOT BEING ABLE TO ENJOY IT WITH OTHERS IS NOT WORTH IT.

Maybe you need to start taking steps to seek out relationships, and that's OK, too. This is a worthy pursuit in my book. During one of the first multiday seminars I taught on the Step principle, I asked everyone in the room to share the steps they had taken from the previous session. I remember listening to people share, but the whole time being distracted because a girl and guy over in the left corner of the room kept nudging each other as if somebody had something to say. Finally, I called them out. "Hey, guys, do one of you want to share a step you've taken?" The guy finally shared that he had asked the girl out as his step! How fun!

There is one more group I want to address in this chapter. You're the people who find yourselves on the other end of the spectrum. Maybe you're not sacrificing enough. Maybe your balance is shifted in the direction of not doing enough to warrant your goal's attention. Most people suffer with procrastination in one form or another. *Nearly a quarter of adults around the world are chronic procrastinators*, according to research conducted by Joseph Ferrari, professor of psychology at DePaul University. Some people procrastinate because they're lazy, but if you're reading this book, I'll bet that you're not the lazy type. You wouldn't have sought out a book like this if you were. You most likely procrastinate because you have a hard time believing you can do it. Or you may find the steps ahead intimidating to a point that renders you unable to move. My belief is that if you are procrastinating, there is a reason behind it and it's not that you're lazy.

This is a great opportunity to break your steps down into even smaller steps. I would rather see you take a "half step" than no step at all. If you find yourself not moving because at the root you are scared of the outcome or you don't believe you can do it—that's OK! Take a smaller step. Maybe you have been dreading sharing your idea with the boss even though you know it's great. How about sharing it with a friend first? Let them give you pointers. Maybe it makes sense to share it with a coworker that you trust in order to get advice. Most of the time there is a step in between the step we are delaying to take. Those half steps can give us the courage needed to take the full step we have been avoiding.

There will come a time when you have to take a risk. Accomplishing anything great requires facing your fears head-on. I have a good friend who recently moved from working at a salon to renting a space of her own. This was a scary move. Would anyone come? Would she be able to make the same amount of money as before or would she lose money? We all face questions like these. When I was first writing this book, I was nervous to share it with anyone because they might think it wasn't good. However, at some point, we have to take the step we fear the most. I promise it's liberating. It feels great to stare fear in the face and do it anyway. In my business roles, I often speak with C-level executives of Fortune 100 companies. It's my job to convince them of our company's ability to help them accomplish their goals. The first time I did this was a pretty nerve-racking experience. I was young, I didn't have a ton of credibility, and I was nervous they would chew me up and spit me out in front of all of my coworkers. How would I ever recover? I did it, though trembling a bit, but I got through it. Now, I've done it a 100 times and I look forward to it. The thing we fear the most may one day be the thing we do the best.

There's no way to get around the fact that at some point we will have to do something uncomfortable. You can do it.

Balance. It's important to the process. Whether you need better balance toward those you love or toward ambition, I challenge you to make it a priority. Without balance you will either accomplish and lose or never accomplish at all.

12
STEPPING IN THE MUD

Sometimes we just get stuck. It's that point when you feel that nothing you are doing is moving you forward and the thought of continuing on is painful. This feeling typically shows up after you've been stepping for a while. Maybe it's a week in, a year down the road, or anywhere in between. On top of the feeling that you're not moving, you start to wonder whether you have wasted the last [fill in the blank] time of your life pursuing something that you will never achieve.

There is some good news: It's normal! What you are experiencing is something that every stepper before and every stepper after you has and will face.

I'll go even further to say that anyone attempting to accomplish something large or small will be confronted with the same challenges.

I'd mentioned earlier that I ran cross-country when I was younger. I'm very fortunate to have been on the team that won a state championship when I was in high school. It is still to this day one of the coolest accomplishments in my life. Distance running makes you push your body to limits you don't feel like you were meant to go, and once you've accomplished something new there is another new goal in front of you. I ran many races, and by the end of each race, I had nothing left and used every ounce of strength to cross that finish line ahead of the competition.

One might think that after conditioning and running for a while a race would be second nature, but the reality is that with every race you push yourself a little bit harder. Our races were about three miles. The first mile was always fast and the last mile was, too. It was that pesky second mile, the middle of the race, where you had to fight with everything inside to keep the pace. This is where the races are won and lost. It's that point where the adrenaline from the start is gone and you are still not close enough to see the finish line. This is the point in achieving our goals where we get stuck, too. Some might refer to this as no-man's-land.

When we start we're full of energy and excitement; it's easy to get going. We also get extra strength toward the end because we can see the finish line and we know our achievement is the result of all our discipline and hard work. It's everything in between that is tough. It's the middle of the road where people give up and let their dreams pass them by. This is where most people quit. This dark space between the start and the finish is your mortal enemy.

You will ask yourself, "What do I do?" many times during your journey. You have three options: You can give up, change course, or keep going. When you distill the options down a bit more, you really have two choices: Give up or keep going. If you change course, it means you're still going. You may make a slight adjustment to your step or give it a stronger push, but you're still moving.

To give up or to keep going. This is the question. Let me put this very gently:

KEEP GOING!!!!!!

This is your moment. This is the time to dig deep. Remember we chose steps for a reason. Steps are doable, they can be bite-size. When you first created your step it seemed so easy, maybe even too easy. Put yourself back in that time and overcome the feelings that are trying to stop you from becoming the man or woman you desire to be.

Look at it this way: If you give up, you'll get everything you never wanted. Don't get everything you never wanted! Keep going, and find yourself moving consistently toward the dreams you were meant to achieve.

It's time to look back at your motivation (the reason behind the goal). It's time to refocus on that reason. Surely being a better mom, dad, husband, wife, provider, innovator, etc., is worth keeping going. Whatever your goal or motivation for that goal, it should be more significant than the feeling of giving up. There was a reason you started to step in this direction. When you made that decision, you valued the outcome of your steps to be more significant than what little or big sacrifice you knew it would take to achieve your goal. If you have a hard time getting that feeling back, make a decision to trust your past self. The self that looked at your life and said, "I want more and I'm willing to spend 15 extra minutes working out or wake up early to write a book." I have a good feeling and you should, too, that your past self was making the right decision and the current self is making a decision based on feelings. It's a decision that you will most likely come to regret in the future should you make it.

Making a decision to stop is making a decision to move away from your dream. If you choose to stop walking toward your goals, you might as well be walking in the opposite direction of them. This is what this looks like:

Instead of being healthy, I'm going to be sick.

Instead of having financial security, I'm going to live without certainty to provide for my family.

Instead of being a great dad, I'm going to settle for just having the title "dad" because of my genetic donation.

Instead of being an example for my kids that anything is possible and they can achieve their dreams no matter the circumstances, I'm going to prove to them that it's not possible.

I could go on and on. These are the decisions we are making when we quit. Whether it is as dramatic as I put it or not, the reality of the situation holds true.

Isaac Newton famously said, "For every action, there is an opposite and equal reaction." The action of quitting drives you further from your goal. Just as the action of stepping brings you closer to it.

The feeling to give up is just that. It's a feeling. Feelings change with the wind. Someone says you look nice and you feel great. The next minute, someone says you're ugly and all of the positive emotions flee for the hills. We as humans have the ability to change our feelings.

> **"**

If you give up, you'll get everything you never wanted.

CHRISCAPEHART.CO

Snap it, remember it, share it.

#STEPBOOK

What does this statement mean to you?
Write it down.

_____

_____

_____

_____

CHRISCAPEHART.CO

Think about it, wrestle with it, do it.
#STEPBOOK

The difference between achieving your goal and living in a perpetual state of disappointment is this moment. Steps have given you the ability to know that you can rise above and keep going. You were made for greatness. You were made to do more. You have everything you need to be everything you desire to be. Making the right decision in these moments could be the straw that breaks the camel's back in your favor.

Dealing with the Mud

All mud was not created equal. Sometimes mud is more like quicksand and other times it's just a slight annoyance that requires a little extra effort to pull your foot out.

Level 1 Mud: The Puddle. Level 1 Mud is what happens when you're walking in the yard and all of a sudden the bottom of your shoe has been suctioned to the ground. I immediately start thinking about the cleaning that's going to be necessary. This mud doesn't scare me and I pull my foot out with little thought or effort. You might find yourself in Level 1 Mud if you skip a day of stepping because your schedule was crazy, or perhaps you've missed a day of healthy eating because of a special event. In these instances, the momentum of our steps and strength we've built through consistency easily give us the power to keep going. We might get a little dirty, but we aren't stuck for long.

Level 2 Mud: The Pit. This is the type of mud you encounter when trying to fetch your golf ball out of what you thought was a small creek, but you discover it's actually a large pit of mud. You walk into it cautiously, feeling the unsteady ground under your feet, but you keep going because it's not that bad. Then, about the time you get close enough to reach your ball, it hits you: You're in the middle of a mud pit. If you move too fast you will fall because it's slick. You're not quite to your ball yet, but you are close. However, you know that one more step toward it might mean a sinkhole. Looking back to dry ground, you realize the trip back will be muddier than the trip thus far. It seems like you're in a lose-lose situation. Do you keep going to get your ball, or do you try to retrace your steps and get out of the mud?

In Level 2 Mud, you're able to continue moving toward your goal of retrieving the ball, but you're not sure if it's worth it. You start to question whether one ball is worth the cost of getting more mud on your shoes. You get frustrated with yourself for getting in the situation in the first place. When I first started working with my current editor, Maria, I was excited. I knew she would challenge me to make the book better. When I received her first set of feedback on the draft I was even more excited. Then I sat down to start addressing the feedback. At first it wasn't that bad, but after several hours had passed and I felt like I hadn't made a dent in the revisions, that nervous feeling started to set in. How could I possibly respond to all of this feedback? I honestly thought the book was in a good place, but after seeing Maria's suggestions I realized I still had a lot of work to do. I was already on track to launch the book a year later than I'd wanted. Would this push it out even further? I found myself staring at the comments, too paralyzed to make any revisions. To give you some context, as I'm writing this I can see comment 173 out in the margin. The comments' complexity varies, but some have taken several hours to respond to. I quickly started to feel like I was in the middle of a mud pit. The ball was close, but now those last few steps between my goal and me seemed a bit more arduous than I originally thought.

What did I do? I took it one comment at a time. I settled myself in the middle of the mud pit of comments that required so much action if I wanted to produce a book I was proud of. I remember sitting on a plane and thinking, "There's only one way I will ever get to that ball." It's one comment at a time and no matter how long it takes me, and how muddy I may get, I'm going to finish what I set out to accomplish.

Level 2 Mud requires us to take a deep breath in the middle of the pit, look around, and make a decision to refocus on the step in front of us. It's more of a distraction than truly being stuck. I could have sat for hours thinking about the enormity of work that lay in front of me or I could start doing the work. The silver bullet to Level 2 Mud is getting back to the core of this book: step.

Everything we want to accomplish will require more effort than we first thought. Don't let the extra effort get you stuck. If I would have counted up the time it was going to take to get through the revisions, it would have been like opening myself back up to staring at the mile. I would have found myself paralyzed. Instead, I refocused on the step.

If you're feeling stuck in a mud pit, look back to Chapter 5 for ideas on how to get out. Remember the antidote to giving up: perspective.

EVERYTHING WE WANT TO ACCOMPLISH WILL REQUIRE MORE EFFORT THAN WE FIRST THOUGHT.

Level 3 Mud: The Sinkhole. This is when you step into a mud hole, sink three feet in, and can't move. It's not that you don't want to move; you literally can't move. Level 3 Mud can take on many forms. It can look like being the owner of a wine bar and getting told your alcohol license couldn't be renewed. Or finding out you were the victim of identity theft right before closing on a new home. Then being told by your lender that you can't get the loan even though you didn't do anything wrong. Level 3 Mud comes in all shapes and sizes, but the effect is the same . . . stuck!

I've found there is only one solution flexible enough to get us out of Level 3 Mud: leverage. We have to look for leverage. Think about every movie you've ever seen where someone is sinking in quicksand. The first thing they do, after screaming of course, is look for a stick or a rope to hold on to. This is the only leverage they can get. If you've ever taken a truck mudding after a rainstorm, you've probably also been stuck. If one of your buddies has a winch, you immediately hook it up and get towed out. If not, you look for a board to stick under your tire. This is leverage and when we are stuck it's the only thing that can help us out.

When you find yourself in Level 3 Mud, look for anything that can provide you leverage. It might be a friend's hand you need to grab in order to pull yourself out. Or it might be a winch in the form of calling in a team of people to consult on your situation. The reality of Level 3 Mud is that you can't get out on your own and you shouldn't try to. You need help and that help will come in the form of other people or other resources. When you find yourself here, stop and look for help. This is the time to send out an SOS. This is the time to admit you can't do it on your own and that's OK. This is when a team can really come into play.

I found myself in a sinkhole while working on the first chapter of this book. I'd had help a few times with thinking and editing, but my test readers still weren't responding well to it. I tried to rewrite and rewrite until I reached a point of exhaustion. I had no creative juices left. I needed help and it came in the form of my development editor, Maria. I remember telling her, "I don't know what to do with the first chapter. I just can't seem to get it right. I need you to take a fresh look." She did and I love where we were able to take it. It's not drastically different than where we started, but it's at a place that I feel proud of. I needed someone else's eyes on it.

I've never seen someone get out of Level 3 Mud on their own. Look for advice, look for those who have gone before, look for a helping hand to pull you out. That is a step in and of itself. The worst thing you can do when you get stuck in the mud is to stay stuck because you aren't willing to look to someone else or something else for advice.

Early on in Stan's career when he was selling cookware door to door, he got stuck. He realized he was making as much as he could without adding more hours into the day, which wasn't quite possible. He wanted to continue to grow his income, so he looked for something he could sell to everyone he had already sold to. He talked to leadership about adding soap or some form of consumable to their product line. His thinking was that if he could only find something to go back to his current customers with, he could leverage the relationships he'd spent so much time to build. The company said no and he was stuck. He found his leverage in the form of a different industry—chemicals. He started selling chemicals because they would get used up on a monthly basis and he could scale his revenue without scaling his time. It was perfect. Leverage came to him in the form of a different company using the same skills he had taken the time to develop.

Every time you feel like stopping, keep moving. In fact, move faster, move stronger and with more velocity. It's that moment in the race when you break the back of your opponents by showing your resolve to push through any pain you're feeling. You are so close, my friend. Keep taking that step and celebrate right after because you have just taken one more step toward your destiny.

You are not trying to become the person you were yesterday, but the person you were meant to be. If you didn't feel stuck at some point, you probably weren't doing something that would make a true difference.

Continue to step when you feel stuck. Continue to step when you feel stuck. Continue to step when you feel stuck.

13
WHEN YOU DON'T STEP

Maybe you are wondering what happens if you don't step. Well, I can help you with that . . .

Nothing . . .

Nothing yet . . .

Still nothing . . .

By now surely something . . . but nope, nothing!

OK, you get it. Something does happen when you don't step, but it's probably not what you wanted to happen. Here are a couple of examples.

Let's take my friends Chase and Cambryn. What if they'd never decided to sell Chase's car or do any of the other things they did to fix their finances? What if they were OK with living in debt and decided they would just continue to pay the bills when they came in, and when they needed something they couldn't afford, they'd use debt to get it? The first few years would have been pretty easy. In fact, they would have enjoyed those years a little bit more. They may have bought a few more goodies for around the house and driven newer cars. Sure, they would still have the nagging payments each month, but who cares?

Let's fast-forward a few years. Cambryn and Chase are about to have their second baby and they really want Cambryn to be able to stay home. At this point they have over $1,500 a month in debt payments between the school loans, cars, and credit cards. It would be a dream for Cambryn to stay at home, but they just can't make it happen so she continues to work. The only problem is they still don't get any further ahead. Between the debt payments, daycare, and growing bills, all of Cambryn's paycheck is pretty much gone. They continue in the cycle.

Fast-forward a few more years. Chase and Cambryn have always dreamed of private school, but there is no way that's happening. Pass on that dream. Forward ahead a few more years. It's time for their first daughter to go to college. They have always wanted to be able to help their kids go to school without debt, but they don't have enough money. They help Paisley take out a loan in order to go to college. In the next four years, Paisley will start her working life with over $100,000 in student loans. This breaks Chase's and Cambryn's hearts because they once again have not been able to give their children the life they want. What could they have done? This is just the way life is. They had debt coming out of school, too. Their kids will be fine, just like they were.

SOMETHING DOES HAPPEN WHEN YOU DON'T STEP, BUT IT'S PROBABLY NOT WHAT YOU WANTED TO HAPPEN.

A few years later, both of their daughters get married. They take out a line of credit on their house to be able to afford the weddings. Chase and Cambryn are just a few years off from retirement age, but their life savings wouldn't be enough to even pay off their debt, much less live on for the next 30 years. Retirement is not in this couple's future anytime soon. Several more years pass and Chase can no longer hold a steady job. He's been replaced by younger workers.

Chase and Cambryn are forced to move in with their children and make them support them. This isn't the life they wanted, but what could they have done?

What about my grandfather? What if he had sat quietly in his chair instead of saying, "I think I could do that?" Nobody could have faulted him for that—after all, he wasn't naturally outgoing.

Stan could have lived his entire life having barely enough and that would have been a very respectable existence. He served his country and he served his family. He could be like the many older men and women I've met who on their deathbed are filled with regret for a life they wished they could have lived. Or he could be like the old-timers who go to the same breakfast spot every morning and complain about how hard life is. How their Social Security and Medicare isn't cutting it. How our political leaders aren't making the right decisions.

If he had never made that one decision and then continued to ride it out I may never have been able to afford college. His kids would have never had the opportunity to spend day in and day out with him without worrying how to pay their bills. I wouldn't have learned the skills necessary to start a business or write this book.

My grandfather with one small decision changed the course of his family forever. I'm three generations past and this benefit is still paying dividends. And it will continue to pay dividends for my children.

If my grandfather hadn't taken these steps, I don't know where I would be.

What about this book? What if I never started taking two hours a week to write this book? I suppose the future on this is yet to be written, but I can tell what I think the difference would be.

I would still have this weight in the back of my mind telling me I have more to give. Saying that my destiny wasn't being fulfilled. I would find myself searching for meaning in my everyday when all I needed to do was take that step. What if I chose not to spend the money necessary to work with a professional editor? The book may have never reached you, the person reading, whose life will be forever altered, and whose kids and grandkids will be the beneficiaries.

What if I hadn't continued the process after a year? I might look my daughter in the face one day when she needs encouragement to go after her dreams and have no basis for my advice to her. She might look me in the face and say, "But, Dad, you never went after your dreams."

What about your story? What would your life look like if you didn't make a decision to step? Maybe you would lose your life early to an unhealthy lifestyle. Maybe you would set your children up for failure. Or maybe you would never make the impact you were meant to make and will never know what you could have done.

WHAT WOULD YOUR LIFE LOOK LIKE IF YOU DIDN'T MAKE A DECISION TO STEP?

I hope this chapter makes you uncomfortable. It makes me uncomfortable every time I read it. It challenges me with the reality that the decisions I make today will have a dramatic impact on my future and the future of other people. I have a responsibility to myself and to them, and so do you.

14
THE MOST POWERFUL STEP

Throughout this book I've talked about taking steps to create a better life for you and for your family. I think this is so important and worth pursuing with an intense strength. But I want to challenge you to step outside the lens of self for a few minutes and talk about steps for others.

I was raised on the principle that it is better to give than to receive. The act of bringing life and hope into another person's life can be more rewarding than accomplishing a goal of your own. I believe that. We all have different backgrounds, different problems, and different resources, but there is one thing I'm fairly certain of: There is someone you could help.

We have to be honest with ourselves about the state of our world. There are the rich, there are the poor, and there is everyone in between. Children in one house are picky eaters and in a house just a few blocks away there may not be enough to eat. Clean water is taken for granted in my household, but in another country it is a mother's prayer for her children.

Many people have access to doctors and medicine while others must face the realities of HIV, cancer, malaria, or some other life-threatening disease without any help. If you are reading this book, there is a good chance you have more than most in the world. I could go on and on with these examples. Sometimes the reality of what children and other men and women across the world go through can seem like too big of a challenge for us to do anything about it. It's just too easy to turn my attention to my own struggles and tune out others' cries.

I'm concerned with my lawn and having granite countertops in the kitchen. I "need" a new car or that TV or couch. Or maybe it's less materialistic than that. It's that I want my children to go to college without debt and I'm fighting to make that happen.

I find that I can easily turn my attention to my problems. The larger I make them the less I'm able to see the needs of others. Friends, I implore you: There is a world that is hurting. There is someone who needs you to take a step in their direction more than you can imagine.

I was recently at an event called "An Evening of Hope." It was a fundraising dinner put on by a nonprofit organization I have been friendly with for a long time, Sower of Seeds. We ate dinner and bought raffle tickets in support of this great cause. Shortly into dinner, we watched a video that told the story of a woman who was the victim of human trafficking.

Today there are somewhere in the neighborhood of 17 million slaves, many of them children. This particular organization works with girls who have been tricked into sex slavery. They are beaten, abused, and made to sleep with 20 or 30 men every night. Some are as young as six years old. The video showed how this organization went undercover into some of the brothels. These women's stories were horrific. One 22-year-old woman risked her life to escape. She jumped out of a building, hurt her leg, and was able to get away. She had nowhere to go, so she fled back to her village to find her family. It had been five years since she was tricked into sex slavery. When she found her family, they would not let her come back into their house because of what she had done. What had she done? She had been drugged, beaten, and forced to have sex with men. She hadn't done anything wrong. After sleeping outside of her parents' house under a tree for several days, she decided it would be better to go back into slavery than to not be loved by anyone.

She walked back to the brothel she had risked her life to escape from and once again became a slave. I'm sitting on my porch drinking a cup of coffee and across the world and even in my own town there are children, women, and men suffering from atrocities I cannot even imagine.

If I'm to be completely honest the stories I hear from different organizations can leave me feeling a bit overwhelmed. I'm deeply touched and saddened by the stories, like I'm sure many people reading this feel, but the hugeness of the situation sometimes leaves us wondering, "What difference can I make? I'm spending every ounce of energy and money I have to provide for my family. I don't think I can help."

Hopefully, by this point in the book you realize where I'm going with this. Roughly 17 million people were not enslaved by one person and 17 million people will not be freed by one person. The U.S. Civil War was one of the most costly and deadly we have ever seen. Over 600,000 Americans lost their lives and $4 trillion were spent to end slavery in America. Freedom is never free, but it starts with one step.

If you do only one thing as a result of reading this book, I hope it is this: Step for someone else. You can change your life one step at a time, and your steps can change someone else's life, too.

According to the nonprofit Compassion International, you can provide food for a person for about a dollar a day. Sower of Seeds calculates that you can provide water for a single person for 30 years with approximately $7, and $150 can support a rescued girl for a month. On and on are the impacts you can make with small amounts of money.

If you have ever seen a commercial from one of these groups, you realize that these nonprofits are trying to help us step. They break down the financial numbers into something that we believe can be impactful. It doesn't have to be financial, either. You can volunteer an hour once a month with a local organization. That may not seem like much, but it's a step and that step over time and combined with others adds up.

The steps we take influence those around us. Parents, children will most likely take similar steps that you take, so your step to help others will be multiplied. A step for someone else doesn't always have to be planned. Over the past year there was a commercial that talked about passing on kindness. It showed someone going out of their way to be kind while a passerby catches a glimpse of it and is then spurred to do something nice for someone else. "Kindness, pass it on" is such a great motto.

You can start by opening someone's door or carrying an elderly person's groceries. Or maybe you can encourage that kid whose head is down because his parents didn't show up at the game.

> ## 66

The act of bringing life and hope into another person's life can be more rewarding than accomplishing a goal of your own.

CHRISCAPEHART.CO

Snap it, remember it, share it.

#STEPBOOK

What does this statement mean to you?
Write it down.

_____

_____

_____

_____

CHRISCAPEHART.CO

Think about it, wrestle with it, do it.
#STEPBOOK

Studies show that acts of kindness have a profound effect on the giver, receiver, and even bystanders witnessing these actions. This isn't just a nice anecdote; it's actually a critical part of accomplishing your dreams.

Acts of kindness have been shown to boost the immune system and increase the production of serotonin. Serotonin is a naturally occurring chemical in the body that promotes feeling good and relieves anxiety. The goal of most antidepressants is to promote serotonin production in our bodies.

Some research suggests that acts of kindness can do even more to improve our life. A 2010 article in *Psychology Today* titled "What We Get When We Give" states:

People who volunteer tend to experience fewer aches and pains. Giving help to others protects overall health twice as much as aspirin protects against heart disease. People 55 and older who volunteer for two or more organizations have an impressive 44% lower likelihood of dying [prematurely]—and that's after sifting out every other contributing factor, including physical health, exercise, gender, habits like smoking, marital status, and many more. This is a stronger effect than exercising four times a week or going to church.

In one Harvard study, a video of Mother Teresa's charity work was shown to 132 students. The researchers tested the S-IgA (immunoglobulin A) present in the students' saliva before and after watching the video. S-IgA is an antibody that plays a vital role in mucosal immunity. After watching the video, the test subjects showed increased levels of S-IgA in their saliva and these levels were sustained for at least an hour.

Just being witness to acts of kindness can create lasting benefits in our lives and the lives of those around us. Our step for someone else has a profound and real impact on us and on others.

I believe that as we step for others we will reap the benefits in our own life. Stepping for others will also increase our ability and desire to step for ourselves. It might feel counterproductive, but we should strongly consider the power this can have in our life.

Stan's entire career was set off by one step he took to sell cookware. What might not be so obvious is that Stan didn't take that step for himself; he did if for his wife. Stan couldn't have cared less about having a new cookware set, but he took that step because he knew his wife wanted one. What started as a small gift for her turned into one of the biggest financial successes of his life. It wasn't until I sat down to write this book that I realized my grandfather's success started out of a desire to give his wife a set of cookware. It's pretty cool when you think about how stepping outside of himself turned him onto a completely new career path.

Once his companies were off the ground, Stan always looked for opportunities to help others through his work. I'd mentioned earlier that one of his motivations for building his businesses was so that his kids could always have a place to work. He extended this opportunity to others as well. Time and again my grandfather would help people by giving them a job. It didn't always matter whether or not they were qualified. In fact, most of the time they weren't, but for Stan that wasn't the point. If he saw someone in financial need, he would find work for them to do. He was a believer that a helping hand was one of the most powerful gifts he had and he was quick to offer it.

Whether it's for a nonprofit or a family member. Whether it's for a need or a desire that someone close to you has, stepping for others is a lifeline to your own well-being and success. Make it a priority.

I'm very thankful for the men and women who give up their lives to help others. There are many men and women who have started nonprofits and completely dedicated their lives to a worthy cause. Those men and women need us to also do something so that their efforts can be multiplied.

I was recently in Tulsa, Oklahoma, visiting my friend Matt Nelson. This friend is the lead pastor at City Church Tulsa, and he and the church have been putting a lot of effort into helping orphans in the city find a home. I was shocked when he told me that if one family in every church in their city would foster or adopt, there would not be a single child without a home. Matt is working in Tulsa to see this happen. It's a fantastic example of how powerful a step can be.

We are the answer to the world's problems. All we have to do is start stepping. Start doing something. We can all do something.

One step that you can take now is to give this book to someone else. If you are the first person to read this copy of the book, you'll find a place in the front to register and name it. If someone has had the book before you, you'll be able to see where it's been by reading the register, like a library book. And much like a library book, this book was made to be passed on from one person to another. You may have been the recipient of this book from someone else. You're benefiting from someone else's step in your direction . . . Pass it along. Let's see how far this book can travel and how many steps it can take.

I leave you to answer the question: Who can I help by passing this book along?

APPENDIX

Breaking Down Your Mile

Study Guide

This is an outline for how you can break down your mile into small steps. Use it as a guide to get you started. See p. 34, "Breaking Down the Proverbial Mile," for details on how to use this method.

What: _____

When: _____

Quantify: _____

If statement (your mile): _____

If _____

Then _____

If _____

Then _____

If _____

Then _____

If _____

Then _____

If _____

Then _____

If _____

Then _____

Example 1

What: I want to start a baby apparel e-commerce business

When: Within one year

Quantify: $10,000 a month in revenue

If statement: If [I want to start a baby apparel e-commerce business that is making $10,000 per month in revenue one year from now] . . .

This is a complex goal with lots of steps. The path toward this goal will be filled with distractions, menial tasks, and all sorts of unexpected events. Having an if statement clearly defined to come back to can help you throughout the process to refine and refocus the steps needed to accomplish the ultimate vision.

Now let's start the process:

If [I want to start a baby apparel e-commerce business that is making $10,000 per month in revenue one year from now] . . .

Then [I need to find product to sell]

Then [I need to talk with baby brands to learn the process for becoming an affiliate]

Then [I need to talk to manufactures about developing custom products]

Then [I need to decide whether I will be a reseller or create a brand with its own products]

With complex miles, there can be lots of steps, and using this process may give you multiple branches of your if–then statement. The above branch is all about the product I'm going to sell. I could continue to flesh that out, but let's take a look at another part of breaking down the mile—the customer.

Then [I need to find people to buy from my website]

Then [I need determine who my target demographic will be]

Then [I need to understand who my target demographic is buying from now]

Then [I need to talk to people in my target demographic to understand what will make them shop from my new store]

Then [I need to create a list of people I know who fall into my target demographic]

Then [I need to see the list of people I know would be willing to buy from my new store]

Then [I need to see if the people who buy from my store will be willing to share their purchase online]

Then [I need to find blogs and social networks that will allow me to advertise to my target demographic]

Now let's look at another branch of this process—financing.

Then [I need to know how much money I will need to invest to get this business off the ground]

Then [I need to find out how much advertising will cost]

Then [I need to find out how much building my website will cost]

Then [I need to know how much money I will need to spend on inventory]

Then [I need to find advisors who have worked in this industry to help me understand the nuances of this business]

Then [I need to put together a budget with projections based on the information I have gathered]

In all three of these sections of breaking down this mile, there has been a consistent theme of research and compiling all the facts needed to start and run this business. Whether you know it or not, the steps in these sections are leading to the development of a business plan. And a business plan is typically the first thing anyone does when creating a business. You may not have known that all of these steps were leading to the creation of a business plan, but the first time you walked in to an investor to share your story and he asked what your plan is, you would be able to walk him or her through the answers to the questions above and they would realize you have done your homework. You have a plan.

Let's expand on this idea a bit more. Let's imagine you are past your initial steps and have been running the business for six months now. Things are going pretty well and you are doing $5,000 per month in business. Let's also assume you are completely overwhelmed because you have real business now, but are still working your full-time job while trying to have some form of a life. There are too many things to get done every day. You have accounting, marketing, shipping, etc. You are struggling to keep this business operating. You want to double the business in the next six months, but you have almost zero time to put into acquiring new customers due to the work created from the current customers. This would be a great time to use your if–then process to break down the mile further.

Then [I need to look at outsourced fulfillment options]

Then [I need to look for a marketing firm to grow my customer base]

Then [I need to be willing to increase my expenses in order to grow] (Note: This may seem like a difficult step, but would be the key to hitting the goal.)

The point is that you can use this process at any phase of the game. An if–then statement may not plot out every single step that you would ever take when starting a business, but it can help you figure out steps when you don't know what to do.

Example 2

Here is another example of using the if–then statement to tackle a complex project—launching a brewery. As with the e-commerce store, there are several miles within this larger project and we can use the if–then process to break down each one. We can also use what, when, and quantify to get the if statement for each mile.

What: I want to start a brewery

When: Within 18 months

Quantify: Bringing in $300,000 in revenue the first year

If statement: If [I want to start a brewery within 18 months that earns $300,000 in revenue] . . .

Mile A: Then [I need to write a business plan]

What: I want to write a business plan for my brewery

When: Within three months

Quantify: That outlines each element of the business and my projected budget

If statement: If [I want to write a business plan for my brewery within three months that outlines each element of the business and my projected budget] . . .

Then [I need to learn how to write a business plan]

Then [I need to read books about how to write a business plan]

Then [I need to research and read other breweries' business plans]

Then [I need to talk to other brewery founders and business owners about how they approached their business plan]

Then [I need to outline each section of my business plan]

Then [I need to pick one section to start writing (The Market)]

Then [I need to do market research on other breweries in my area, and other breweries that distribute to the areas in which I would like to sell my beer]

Then [I need to start writing the next section (The Budget)]

Mile B: Then [I need to find a space for the brewery]

What: I want to find a space for my brewery

When: Within six months

Quantify: That is big enough for brewing equipment, storage, an office, and a tasting room

If statement: If [I want to find a space for my brewery within six months that is big enough for brewing equipment, storage, an office, and a tasting room] . . .

Then [I need to think about how big the space needs to be to fit everything I need]

Then [I need to figure out how much we can budget for rent]

Then [I need to find a real estate agent who can help me find spaces within our budget and specifications]

Then [I need to visit each space]

Then [I need to figure out how much work it would require to build a brewery in each space]

Then [I need to see if the costs for building a brewery in each space will fit our budget]

Then [I need to consider other factors for each space, like location, aesthetics, and the landlord's temperament]

Then [I need to find out whether the space I want will be available when we're ready to build the brewery]

Then [I need to put in a lease application for the space I want]

Then [I need to sign a lease and leave a deposit]

Mile C: Then [I need to find investors]

What: I want to find investors for my brewery

When: Within six months

Quantify: To provide the $400,000 start-up funds we need to launch the brewery

If statement: If [I want to find investors for my brewery within six months to provide the $400,000 start-up funds we need to launch the brewery] . . .

Then [I need to complete my business plan]

Then [I need to research and learn the mechanics of how a business owner brings in investors]

Then [I need to find a lawyer to help me draw up papers for investors]

Then [I need to find potential investors]

Then [I need to ask friends and colleagues if they know anyone who might be a potential investor]

Then [I need to meet with each potential investor and share my vision and business plan with them]

Then [I need to follow up and confirm whether they'd like to invest]

Then [I need to send paperwork to the people who agree to invest]

Example 3

What: I want to finish my master's degree

When: Within two semesters

Quantify: 36 credit hours

This is an example that came up with when I was taking a group of young professionals through the concepts in this book over several months. One gentleman came to the front of the group and started to break down this mile. A couple of interesting caveats to note are that he had a full-time job and was doing this through online and night classes.

If statement: If [I want to take 36 credit hours in two semesters] . . .

Then [I need to take 18 credit hours each semester]

Then [I need to sign up for 18 credit hours]

Then [I need to find 18 hours of time in my week]

Then [I need to consider five hours of homework per class per week]

Then [I need find 90 hours in my week to devote to school]

Then [I need to block those hours on my calendar]

You may be able to guess where this is going. Within five minutes, it became very obvious to everyone that this was not a reality under his current circumstances. When you are going through this process, you may set an aggressive goal like this gentleman, and there is nothing wrong with that. However, there are times where you might want to consider revising your "when."

I explained to him that unless he was able to become a full-time student, two semesters was probably not the right goal. After looking at this he revised his timeline and we went through the process again.

The point here is that breaking down your mile will also help you identify areas in your dream or goal that may need to be refined. This is an OK and important part of the process.

Example 4

What: I want to lose weight

When: Six months

Quantify: 25 pounds

If statement: If [I want to lose 25 pounds in six months] . . .

Then [I need to lose five pounds a month]

Then [I need to lose approximately 1.2 pounds per week]

Then [I need to research diet programs that can help me lose 1.2 pounds per week]

Then [I need to start eating off the light menu]

Then [I need to start blocking 15 minutes a day to do some form of exercise]

Then [I need to start drinking coffee without creamer or sugar]

Then [I need to drink two glasses of water at every meal before having anything else to drink]

We've found several steps that someone could quickly start taking toward this goal. Whether you take all or some of these steps is completely up to you, but you are building your playbook for breaking down your mile.

ACKNOWLEDGEMENTS

I've never accomplished anything great without a team. I feel incredibly blessed to be able to say with utter confidence that this book was brought to life only through the encouragement, hard work, and passion of the team I feel honored to have worked with.

Maria Gagliano, Thank you for helping me develop my idea into the book it is today. Working with you has been one of the best experiences in my life. I couldn't be prouder of the book and that is a direct reflection of your influence. Thank You!

Ronnie Johnson, Thank you for the 6 a.m. mornings and the passion you put into designing a beautiful brand and book. Your extra effort and care made what we have today possible.

Marcus Ryan, Thank you for being a sounding board, advisor, challenger, and anything else I needed in the process. You gave freely and generously. Thank you!

George Thomas, Thank you for the advice, the effort and the person you have been to me throughout this process. I'm extremely grateful and better because of it.

Jennifer Eck, Thank you for your effort and care while working on this project.

Johan and Hannah Etsebeth, Thank you for being the first people I trusted to read anything I had written. You have both generously given of your time and advice throughout the process.

Michael and Selah Hirsch, Thank you for continuing to encourage, offer support, and technical help in a moments notice. I'm honored that you would give so much of your time to help my dream come true.

Ryan Moede, Thank you for your overwhelming generosity, talent and speed with helping me on some of the finishing touches.

The Stories

To those who've allowed me to use their story in the book; Thank you for following your dreams and letting me share them with the world. This book is richer because of them.

Chase and Cambryn Willsey

Jon and Trina Mitchell

Craig and Erin Conner

Ian McConnell

Celia Johnson

Matt Nelson

Friends

Thank you to all of my friends who have encouraged and supported me in numerous ways. There are more of you than I can list. I'm eternally grateful for your friendship.

Thank you Micah Davis and Ethan Fisher. Two of my best friends through thick and thin. The contributions you've made to my life and in consequence this book are immeasurable.

Family

I may end my acknowledgement with family, but not for a show of how important they have been to everything I have and will accomplish. I have an amazing family from every side. I have been supported, encouraged and continually given love like many may only dream about. We don't get to choose our family, but I wouldn't have chosen differently. Thank you all for your hard work in making me into the person I am today. I hope you can see my work as an accomplishment of your own. You are littered throughout the pages of this book and live with me; even the ones that are gone. I am the man I am because of the family I have. Thank you, Thank you, Thank you.

INDEX

ABOUT STEP

We don't know each other, but I'll dare to guess we have at least one thing in common: Who we are today is not who we want to be tomorrow.

The reality is that we are busy. We have work, bills, families, and the list goes on of things that not only compete but demand our time. It's easy to let our dreams fade into oblivion because we don't see how we could possibly accomplish them.

Step is about reclaiming, pursuing and achieving those dreams in the midst of everyday life. In fact, the book was written to prove this very concept. The author used the principles you'll learn about to write and launch Step while successfully doubling the size of a technology company, being the father to a two year old and the husband to his wife.

When you read Step you will start to dream again and if you are already dreaming you will be encouraged and equipped to continue the journey you're on.

Remember the mile may be long, but the step is short!

ABOUT THE AUTHOR

Chris Capehart is a serial entrepreneur, speaker, author and encourager of all things GREAT! Chris' childhood was anything but typical. Instead of the usual after school activities, Chris spent his free time working in the family "startup" business.

That startup went on to gross over 200 million dollars in sales. Chris got the education of lifetime before he had even started high school.

Over the years since, Chris has experienced success and failure in business. He's started or had ownership in over 10 ventures. Having lost his mother to suicide and father to cancer, his experience in defeating the odds reaches beyond the business world.

Through the highest of highs and lowest of lows, Chris has learned a handful of principles that have shaped who he is and will become. As he likes to say, "We are always becoming someone."

Chris is currently a part of one of the most innovative technology companies in the country which recently had an app ranked #1 in the iTunes App Store. His leadership has helped the company to continue it's pace of doubling year over year while also launching new divisions.

Find out more at

CHRISCAPEHART.CO

@chriscapehart
facebook.com/chriscapehartco
instagram.com/chriscapehart
linkedin.com/in/chriscapehart